MIXED MEDIA Jewelry Techniques

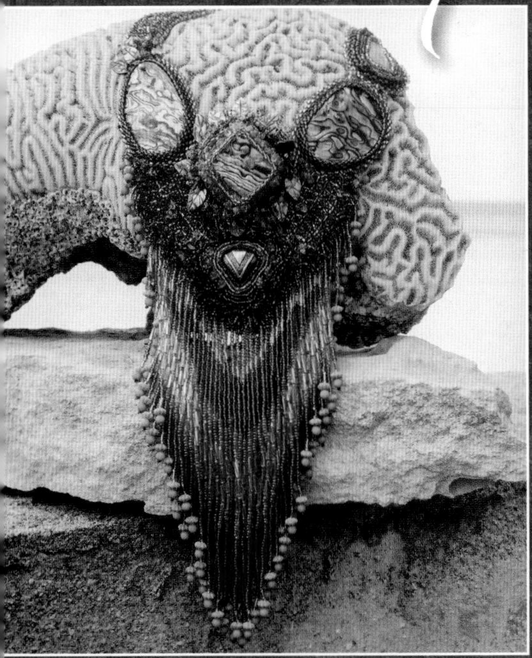

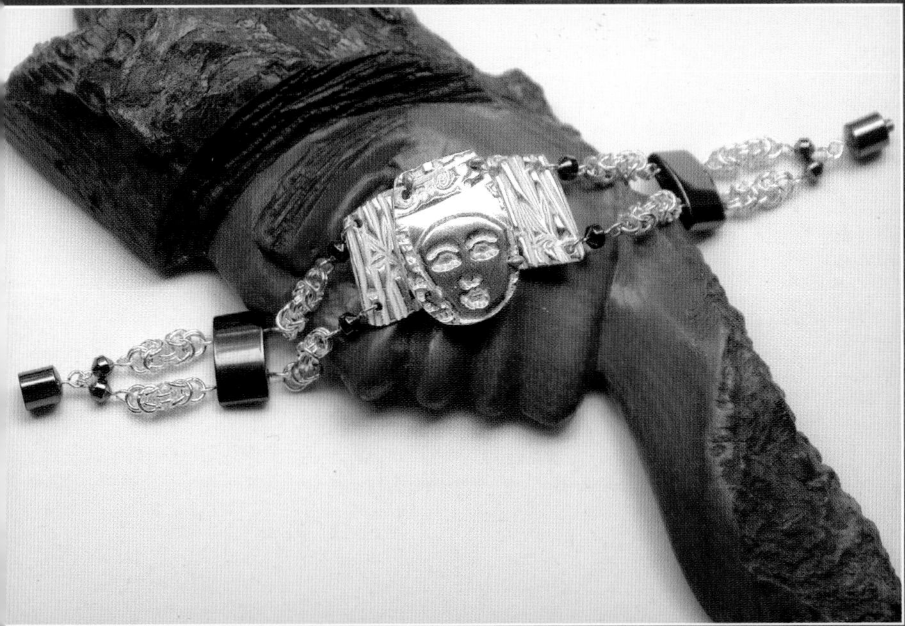

Lana May & Her Friends

Schiffer Publishing Ltd

4880 Lower Valley Road, Atglen, PA 19310

Library of Congress Control Number: 2009937874

Designed by John P. Cheek
Cover design by Bruce Waters
Type set in Humanist 521 BT/Zurich BT

ISBN: 978-0-7643-3429-0
Printed in China

Schiffer Books are available at special discounts for bulk purchases for sales promotions or premiums. Special editions, including personalized covers, corporate imprints, and excerpts can be created in large quantities for special needs. For more information contact the publisher:

Published by Schiffer Publishing Ltd.
4880 Lower Valley Road
Atglen, PA 19310
Phone: (610) 593-1777; Fax: (610) 593-2002
E-mail: Info@schifferbooks.com

For the largest selection of fine reference books on this and related subjects, please visit our web site at
www.schifferbooks.com
We are always looking for people to write books on new and related subjects. If you have an idea for a book please contact us at the above address.

This book may be purchased from the publisher.
Include $5.00 for shipping.
Please try your bookstore first.
You may write for a free catalog.

In Europe, Schiffer books are distributed by
Bushwood Books
6 Marksbury Ave.
Kew Gardens
Surrey TW9 4JF England
Phone: 44 (0) 20 8392 8585; Fax: 44 (0) 20 8392 9876
E-mail: info@bushwoodbooks.co.uk
Website: www.bushwoodbooks.co.uk

Acknowledgments

Dale "Cougar" Armstrong

Seed bead designer and teacher, Lana May has gathered together an intimate group of instructors, who conduct classes at the J.O.G.S. Gems show in Tucson, Arizona, every February. Our tightly knit group includes multi-award winning jewelry designers in a variety of media such as seed beads; wire; polymer clay; beads; metals; glass lampworking, and PMC, (Precious Metal Clay). While enjoying a dinner together in 2008, someone brought up the idea that we should collaborate to write a book that would combine our various media into unique designs. Such a book would be written to encourage studio jewelers to begin associating with peers having different jewelry making skills, combining design ideas, and creating exciting new pieces together. The result is the book that you are presently reading.

Working in our own studios, located around the United States, and communicating via email and telephone conversations, each of us are regular women who have family and household responsibilities as well as our work with jewelry. It is due to the amazing support and encouragement of our families that we are able to do what we do! As such we would especially like to thank our spouses, who put up with late night phone calls, help with the laundry and childcare, occasionally make dinner, don't complain about nights when we don't get to bed until long after they are asleep, do yard, garden and home maintenance (sometimes even housework!), and share us with the rest of the world as we endeavor to continue our creative passions.

- To Phillip May and Grygoriy from Lana: "Thank you for what you have done and still doing for me."
- To Charlie Armstrong from Dale "Cougar:" "As I try to say often, thank-you so much for lovingly letting me spread my wings and fly! Now, let's go cut rocks."
- To Ken Bjornson from Meredith: "Your constant support is amazing to me! XXOO"
- To Leonard Sheiba from Irina Serbina: "For your wisdom, patience, and kindness"
- To Alex Bugrimenko from Olena: "For full support and love always!"
- To Cornell Cook from Geri: "No one could have a better supporter of their dreams than me! Thanks for your continued encouragement and help in everything I do."
- To Peter Manning and Anya from Albina: "For all your love and encouragement."

This book was written for all of our students; those past, present and those we will meet. Enjoy what you do and share your passion!

The materials used throughout the book were provided by Fire Mountain Gems and Beads

Contents

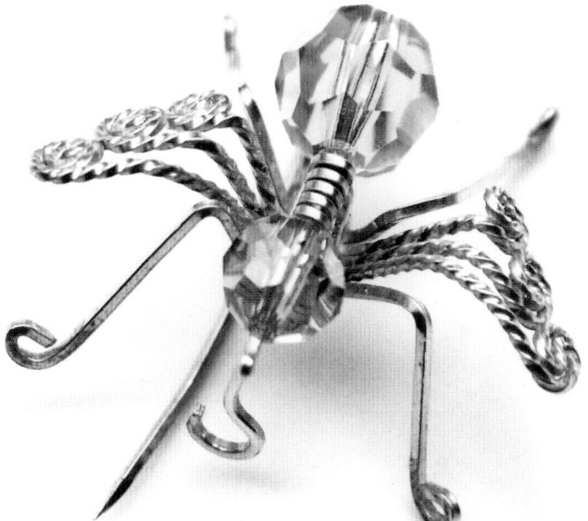

Project 1.

Summer Set

Dale "Cougar" Armstrong, Lana May,
& Olena Bugrimenko

Techniques: *wire work, beading technique, and chain maille*

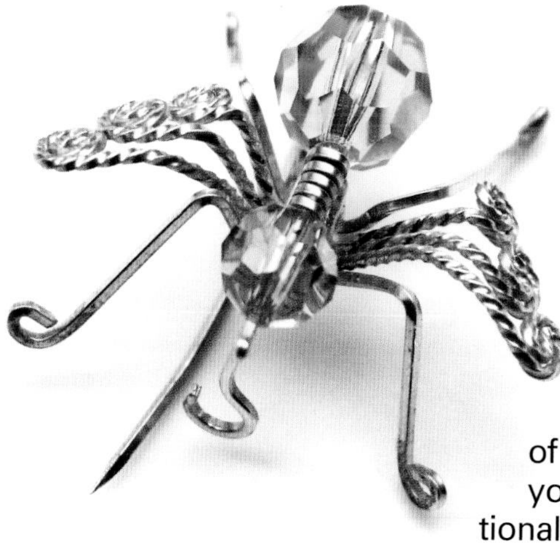

Buzzy Bees Scatter Pin

Dale "Cougar" Armstrong

Scatter whimsical sparkle with these adorable bee pins. The bee has long been admired and revered as an example of being able to do the impossible. Follow these directions and you can create your own beautiful, little bees to give as inspirational gifts, or wear one yourself as a reminder that YOU can do *anything*!! Be creative by changing the colors and media of the beads used; gemstone beads such as tiger-eye combined with gold wire make a more realistic creature, while faceted pastel crystals make one worthy of being in any fairy tale. (You could even attach a small dangling flower to its nose.)

Materials and Tools

- 22 gauge square, 1/2 hard wire
- 1 – 6mm round or faceted bead
- 1 – 8mm round or faceted bead
- Flat-nose pliers
- Round-nose pliers
- Chain-nose pliers
- Angle cutters
- Pin vise
- Quilter's tape
- Mm/inch ruler
- Extra fine point marker

Instructions

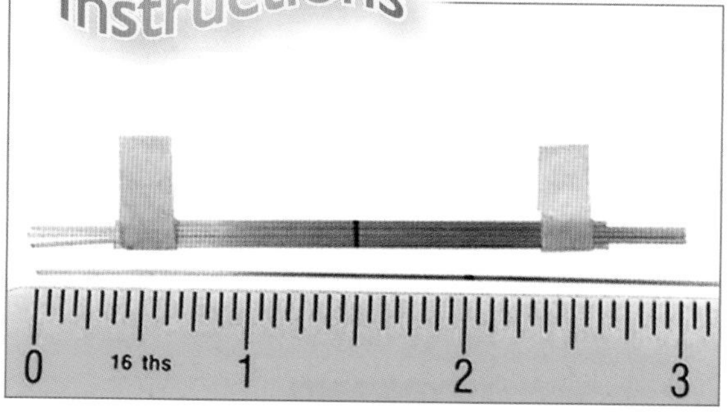

Step 1. Straighten, clean, and then cut 22-gauge square, 1/2 hard wire into the following lengths:

Body = 1pc – 5-1/2 inches
Legs = 2pc – 2-1/2 inches
Wings = 3 pc – 3 inches
Wrap wire = 1pc – 1-1/2 inches.

Above: Center the wing wires between the legs wires and tape near either end. Measure and mark the center of this new bundle.

Below: Measure from one end of the body wire and mark at 2 inches.

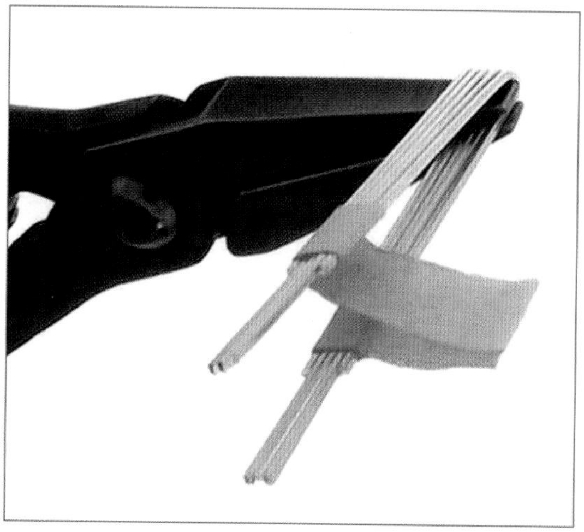

Step 2. At center mark of wing/leg wire bundle, use flat-nose pliers to make a squared U-shape, completely over the jaw of the pliers.

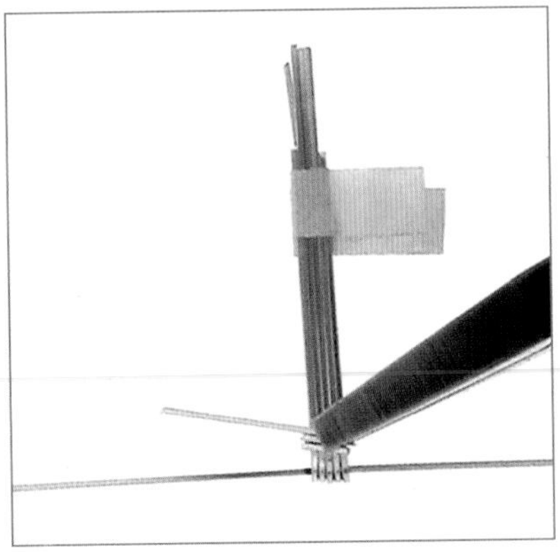

Step 3. Use flat-nose pliers to crimp the U-ed bundle over the body wire on the longer side of the 2-inch mark. Make a deep hook at one end of the wrap wire and use it to wrap the U-ed shape over the body wire, 3 times to show, then trim. Snug the wraps as close to the body as possible.

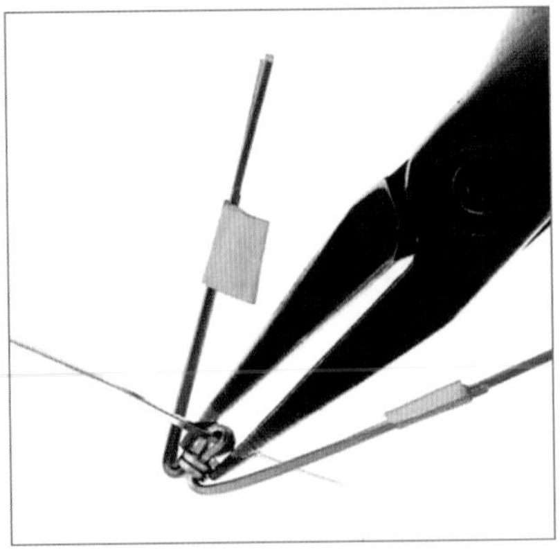

Step 4. Hold the wrapped segment with flat-nose pliers and bend the wings/legs up over the body wire. Remove tape.

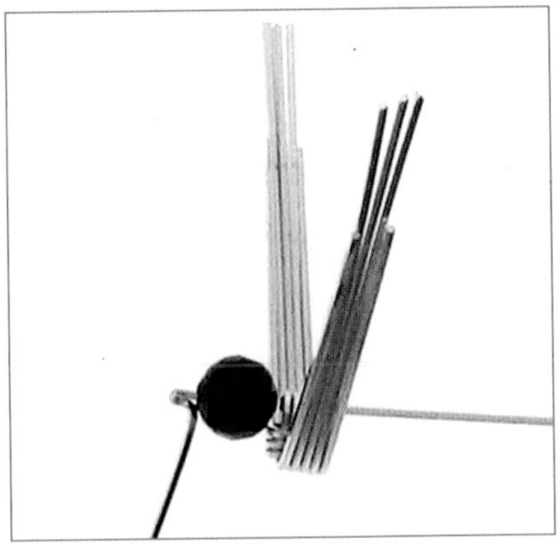

Step 5. On the short end of the body wire, thread on a 6mm bead. Then place chain-nose pliers onto the body wire and hold it, immediately after the bead. Bend the body wire after the pliers' tips, down at a 90° angle. Fold this wire back onto itself, and then down again, forming a *nose*.

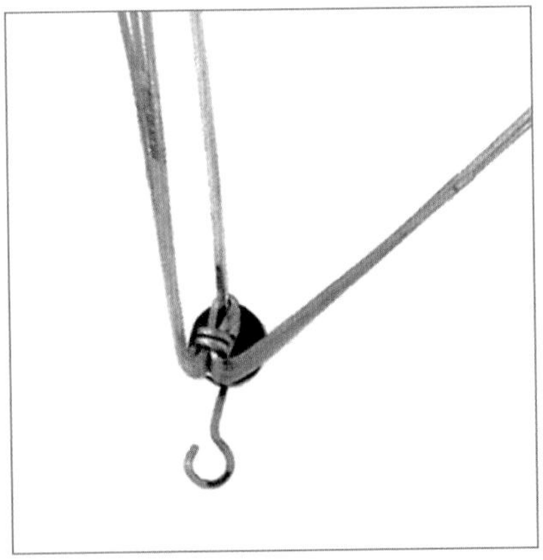

Step 6. Trim this nose wire to 1/2-inch long and use round-nose pliers to make an "eye" to catch the pin.

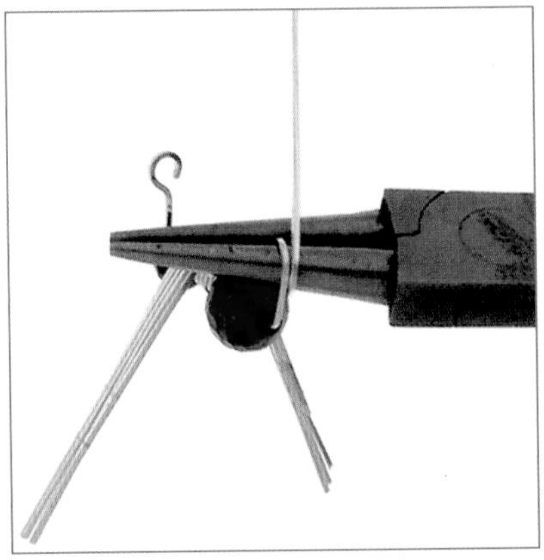

Step 7. On the long end of the body wire, thread on an 8mm bead and bend the body wire down at a 90° angle, locking the bead in position.

Place round-nose pliers, about midway up the jaw, onto the bent body wire, immediately under the bead, and bend the body wire around 1-1/2 times, ending with the wire headed toward the front of the pin. (This forms the pin's spring.)

Step 8. Use flat-nose pliers to properly position the spring directly under the body. Clasp the wire into the formed eye, trim to desired length at a *very* sharp angle and use a file or stone to remove any burrs from the end, forming the pin.

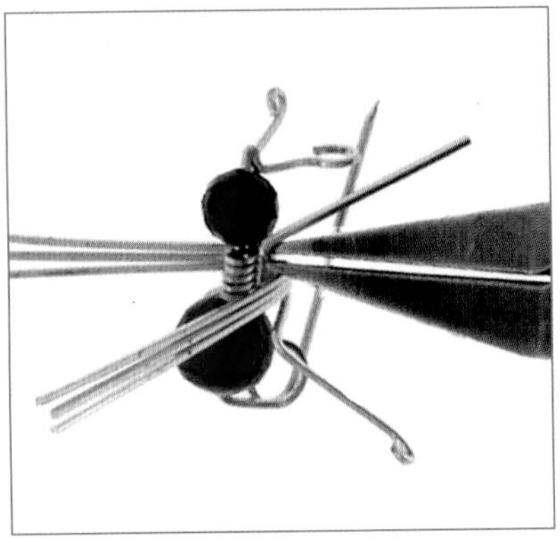

Step 9. Slightly separate the four leg wires from the wing wires. Use flat-nose pliers to hold each leg wire near the body, and with fingers, bend each leg into the position desired, making a knee. At the end of each leg, use chain-nose pliers to roll up each end, forming a foot.

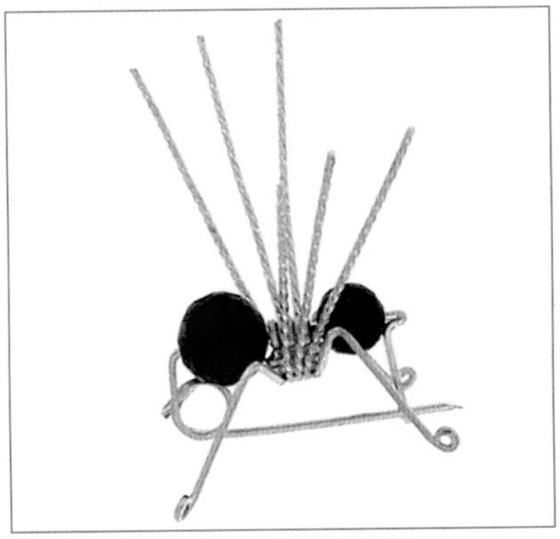

Step 10. Gently fan the wing wires apart and use a pin vise to twist each one. Starting with the wing wire closest to the 6mm bead/head, trim them to the following lengths: 1 inch, 7/8-inch, and 3/4-inch, (the wire closest to the back/body).

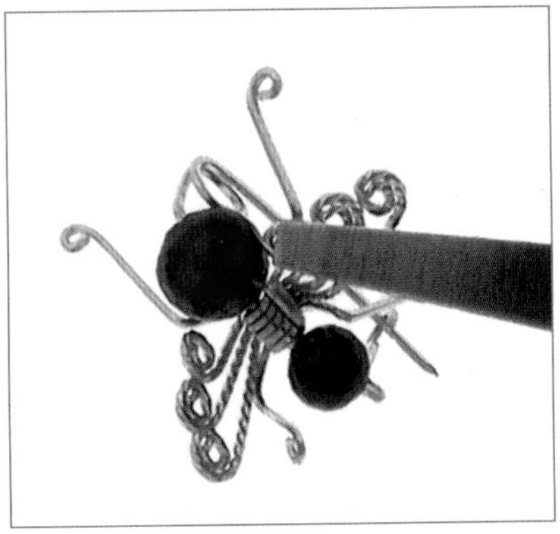

Step 11. Rosette each wing wire toward the side of the body, starting with the shortest and working forward to the longest. Then use flat-nose pliers to shape and position the wings.

Ox-Eye Daisy

Lana May

Materials and Tools

- Yellow seed beads, size 11/0 3gr;
- Yellow seed beads, size 6/0 3gr;
- White seed beads, size 11/0 12gr;
- Needle size #10;
- Fire Line, 6-lb

Instructions

Beading pattern for the center of the daisy.

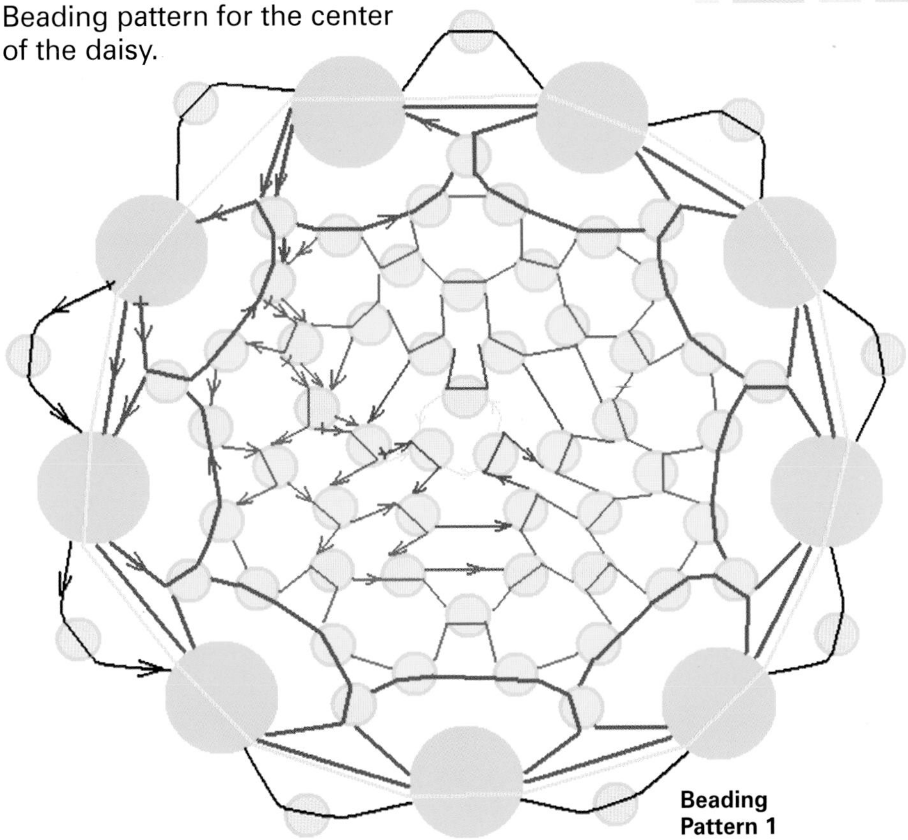

Beading Pattern 1

Step 1. Thread the needle (36in). Pick up nine beads, size 6/0. Make the circle. *[Grey color on Beading Pattern 1].* Leave thread length of 17-18in.

Step 2. Use seed beads, size 11/0, for following steps.

Pick up 4 beads. Pass through two beads, size 6/0. Make arch around first beads size 6/0.

Pick up 3 beads. Pass through last beads from first arch and two size 6/0 beads

Again pick up 3 beads. Pass through last beads from second arch and two size 6/0 beads. Continue this technique for all size 6/0 beads. The last time pass through two size 6/0 beads and one bead from first arch. Pick up two size 11/0 beads. Pass through last bead from prevision arch and the size 6/0 bead from the circle. *[Green line on Beading Pattern 1]*

Step 3. Pass up through two size 11/0 beads from Step 2. Pick up one bead. Pass through next two beads from step 2. Again pick up one bead. Continue pick up one bead after next two beads. (Red line on beading pattern).

Step 4. Last time pass through last two beads from Step 2 and one bead from step3. Pick up one bead between each bead from Step 3. (Blue line on beading pattern).

Step 5. Last time pass through bead from Step 3 and first bead from Step 4.
Pick up one bead. Pass through bead from prevision row. Again pick up one bead. Pass through next two beads from prevision row.
Repeat three times. (Brown color on beading pattern).

Step 6. Pass trough first bead from Step 5. Pick up one bead. Pass through two beads from prevision row. Repeat three times. (Purple color on beading pattern). Pass through three beads from Step 6 two times. (grey color on beading pattern). Make knot between beads on the thread. Cut thread.

Step 7. Turn work over. You see size 6/0 beads. Thread the needle. Pick up one white, size 11/0 bead. Pass through next size 6/0 bead. Pick up one bead between all the size 6/0 beads.

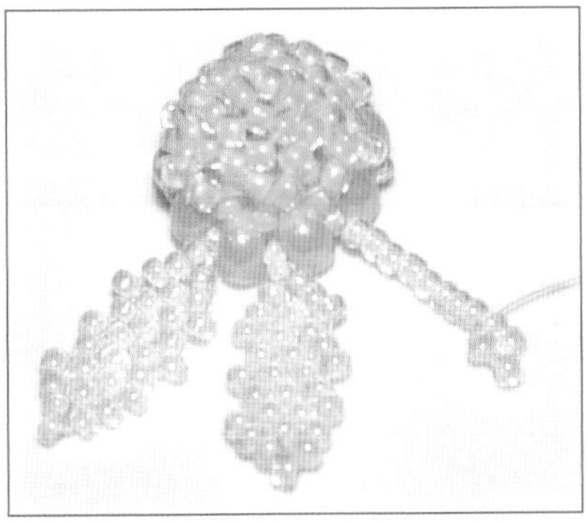

Lower petals.

Creating the Lower Petals

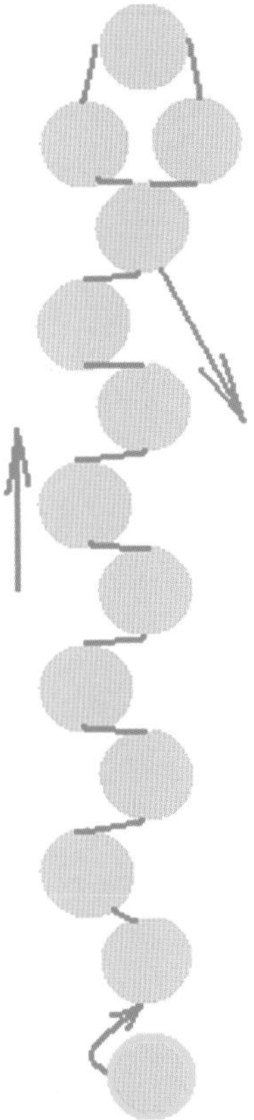

Step 8. Pass through first white bead. Use only white, size 11/0 seed beads. Pick up 12 beads. Pass back through the 4th bead.

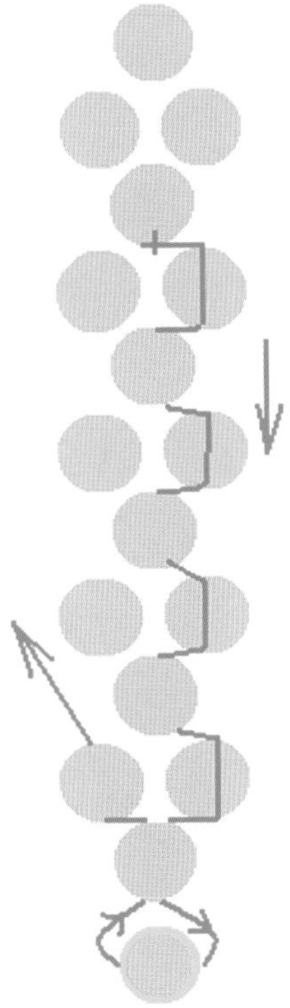

Step 9. Pick up one bead. Skip one bead and pass through next. Continue a peyote stitch. Last time pass through first bead, bead between size 6/0 beads. Pass up through first and second beads.

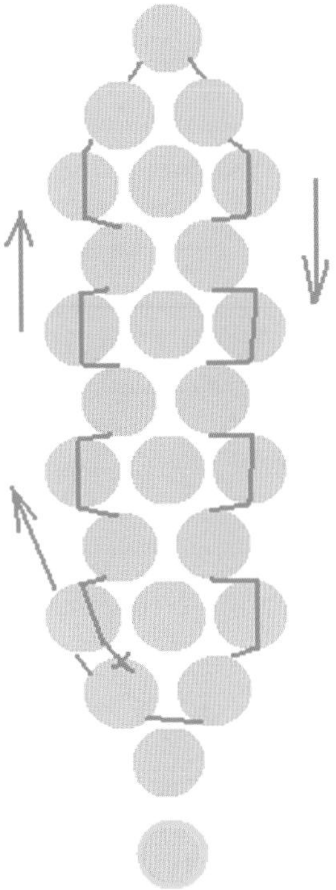

Step 10. Again continue the peyote stitch (go up). Last time pass through three top beads. Continue peyote stitch on opposite side petal (go down). Pass through two beads down and two beads up.

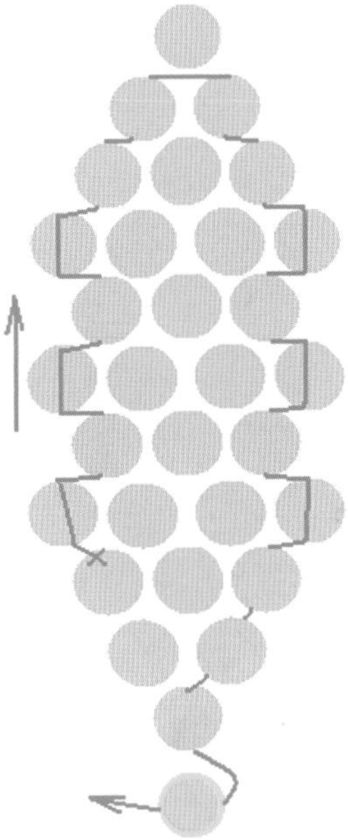

Step 11. Continue peyote stitch. Then pass through two beads up and two beads down on opposite side petal. Continue peyote stitch on this side petal. The last time pass through three seed beads from peyote stitch and bead between the size 6/0 beads. Then pass through the next size 6/0 bead and white beads.

Step 12. Make petals on the beads with green points (green line). Repeat steps 8, 9, 10, and 11 nine times. You will have 9 lower petals.

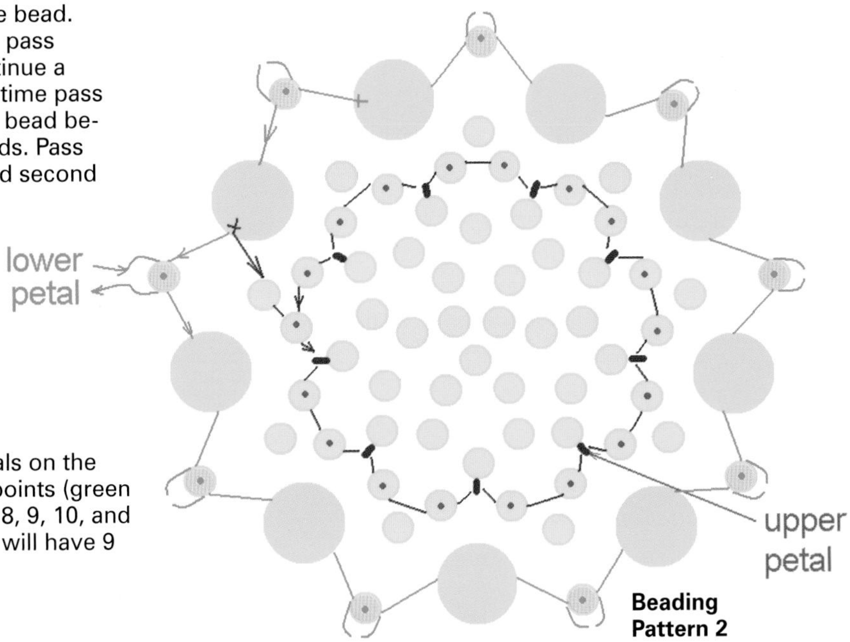

Beading Pattern 2

Creating the Upper Petals

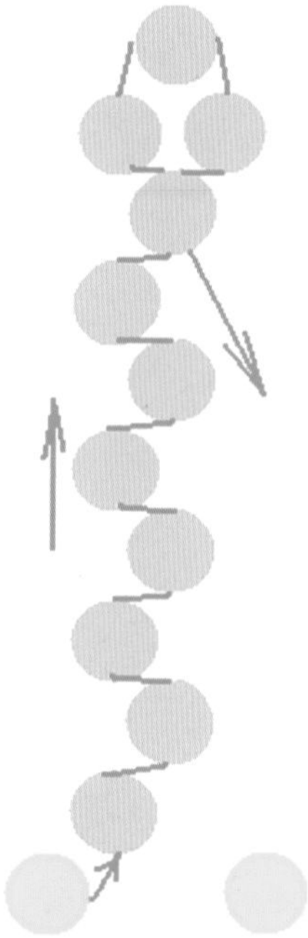

Step 13. The upper petals are smaller, but are made in the same way. Pass through a yellow bead on the inner flower (see Step 12, yellow beads with red dots). Use only white, size 11/0 seed beads. Pick up 11 beads. Pass back through the 4th bead.

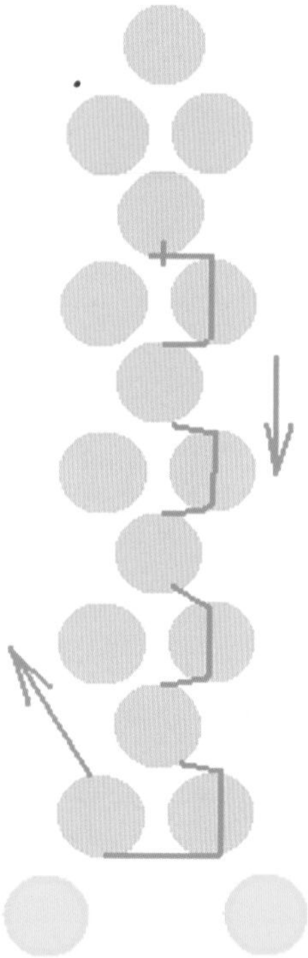

Step 14. Pick up one bead. Skip one bead and pass through next. Continue a peyote stitch. Last time pass through first bead.

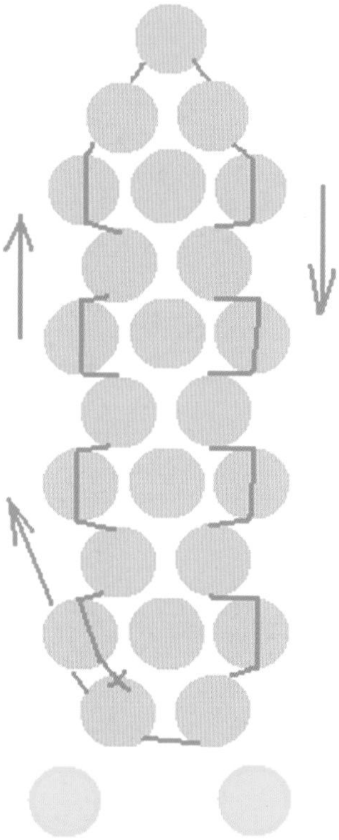

Step 15. Again continue the peyote stitch (go up). Last time pass through three top beads. Continue peyote stitch on opposite side petal (go down). Pass through two beads down and two beads up.

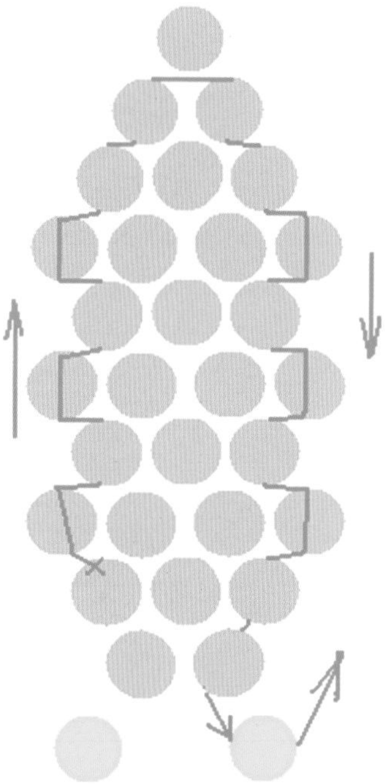

Step 16. Continue peyote stitch. Then pass through two beads up and two beads down on opposite side petal. Continue peyote stitch on this side petal. The last time pass through two seed beads from peyote stitch and through the next yellow bead in the flower center. Make the next upper petal. There are 9 upper petals

Upper petals. Use the same technique for upper petals. See **Beading Pattern 2** and make upper petals between every two beads with red points. (Black line). Look picture of steps 15, 16, 17, 18, and 19.

Summer Bracelet

Olena Bugrimenko

Materials and Tools

- Jump rings 5mm 18ga
- Headpins
- Beads
- Swarovski crystals
- Clasp
- Pliers
- Jump ring tool

Instructions

Step 1. Take four closed silver rings and one open silver ring. Put the four rings onto the open one, and close the ring.

Step 2. Take another open silver ring and put two closed ones onto it. Then put the open ring through the last two closed rings from step 1.

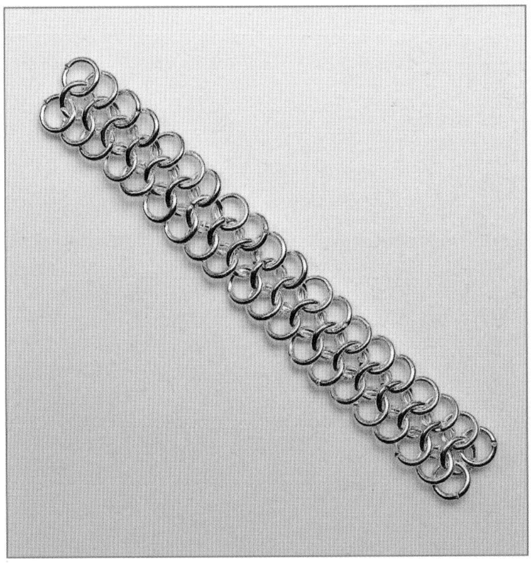

Step 3. Repeat step 2 until there is 19 small silver rings in the middle.

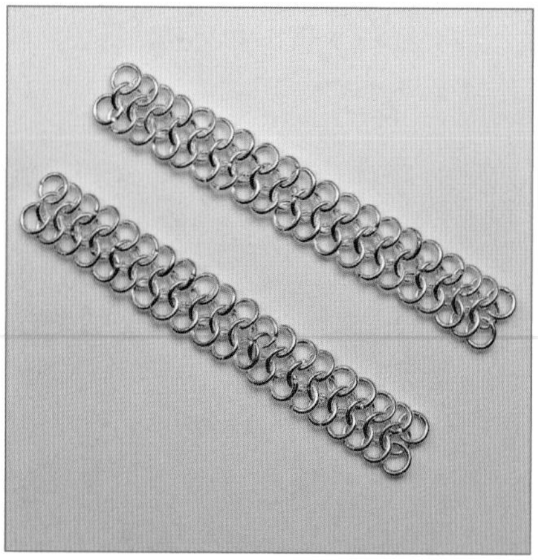

Step 4. Repeat steps 1-3 until you have a replica of the first chain

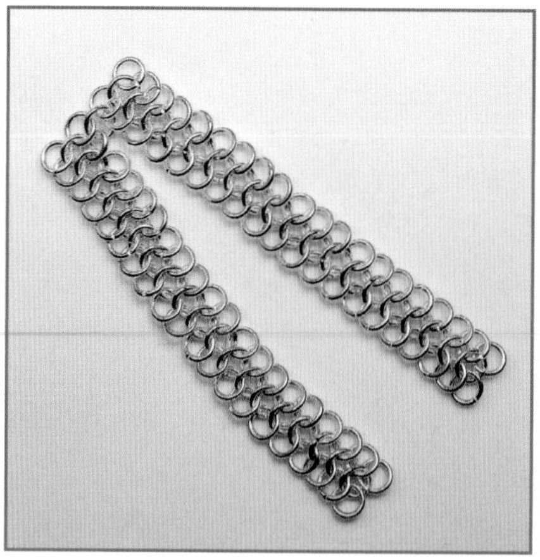

Step 5. You now have to combine the two chains. To do this, take a small open silver ring and put it through the two end rings of each of the chains.

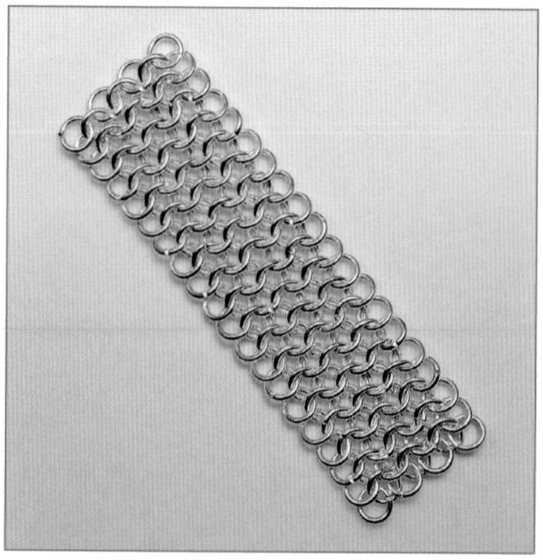

Step 6. Repeat step 5 until you have completely combined the two chains.

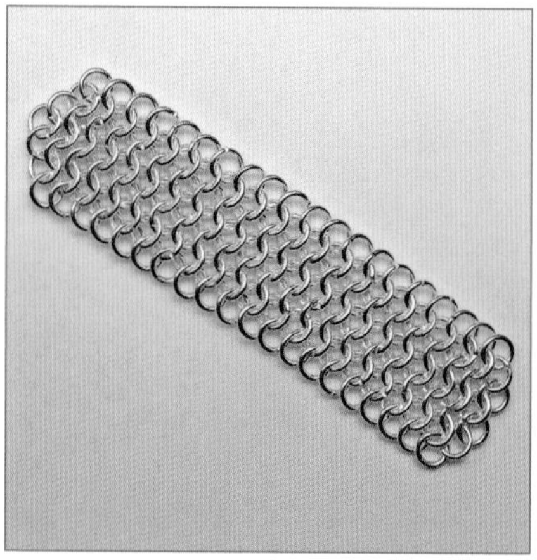

Step 7. Now you have to round the bottom and top part of the chain. To do this, add three small silver rings to the bottom, and two more to the three. At the top, you have to add three small silver rings, then two to the three, and one to the two. This is now one side of the bracelet!

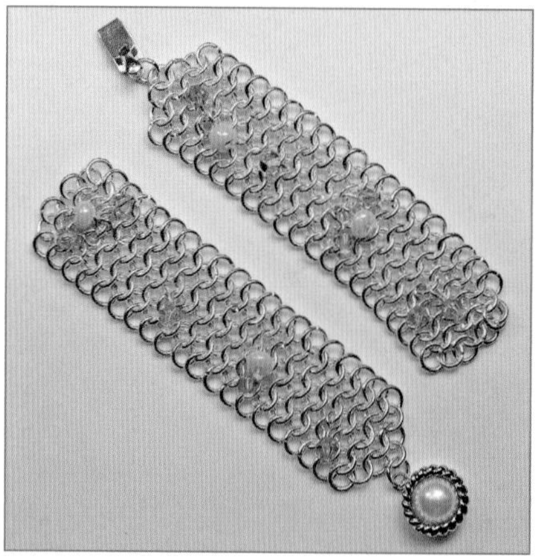

Step 8. You have to make the other side of the bracelet so repeat steps 1-7. Next, add beads and crystals onto the middle rings of each chain. You have to add the pieces of the lock to the one ring at the top of each chain segment that you added in step 7.

Step 9. On the underside of the flower, attach two small silver rings opposite each other on the yellow 6/0 beads. Now, attach the side segments of the bracelet to the two small silver rings you just attached!

You have now created the bracelet!

Summer Necklace

Olena Bugrimenko

Materials and Tools

- Seed beads, 10/0 yellow
- Seed beads, 10/0 green
- Seed beads, 10/0 white
- Seed beads, 10/0 silver
- Bead cup
- Headpin
- Swarovski crystal
- Clasp
- Hook US10/1.15MM
- Pliers

Instructions

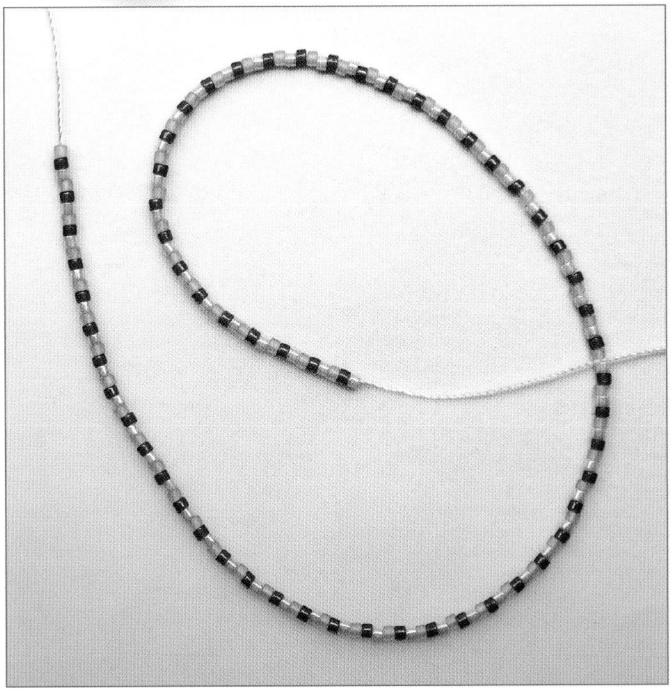

Step 1. For the necklace, you need two tube crochets. Let's make the first one. After putting a needle on the end of a thread, follow the pattern (one yellow, one green, one white) and load all the beads onto the thread. There will be 6 beads around the tube, so you need to get about 102 inches of beads on the thread to get 17 inches as your finished product. Do not cut the thread after you have put on all the beads!

Step 2. Make a slipknot on the hook.

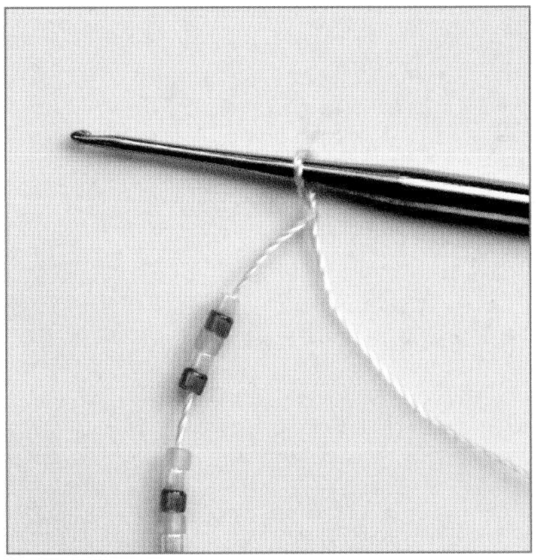

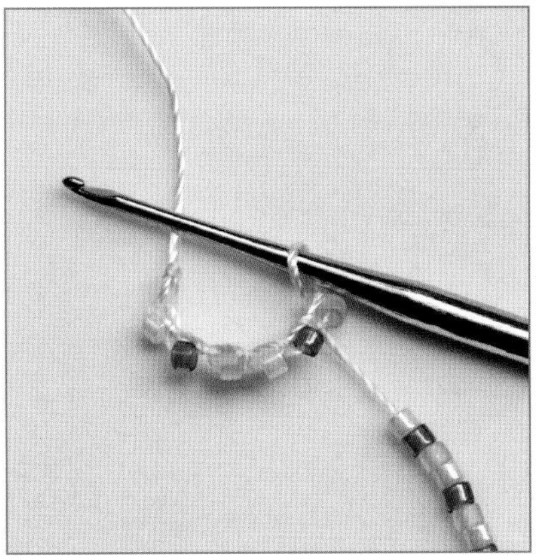

Step 3. Make one chain stitch without using any beads, and six chain stitches, each with one bead.

Row 1:

Step 4. Insert the hook into the first beaded chain, and then slide the bead over to the far side of the hook. Slide a bead down the thread so it sits directly on top of the bead you just moved to the far side of the hook. The thread should come from the right of the bead you just moved to the far side of the hook. When the bead is positioned, wrap the thread over the hook. Pull the thread through the loops. Always make sure that the bead under the hook is the same color as the one being added on.

Step 5. Repeat step 4 until you have finished your second row. Keep repeating step 4 until you have reached your desired length.

Row 2:

Step 6. If you are holding what you've made so far vertically, then the stitched beads lie in a vertical position and the unstitched beads stand up in a horizontal position.

Step 7. When you reach your desired length, you need to make one last circuit but without any beads, just using the thread! Cut the thread, leaving about 5-6 inches of plain thread. You can then hide the leftover thread inside the necklace. Attach headpins to both of the ends of the tubes.

Row 3:

Step 8. Attach a bead cup onto the headpin, add a Swarovski crystal, and make a wrapped loop. Do this to both ends.

Step 9. You have now created the first tube!

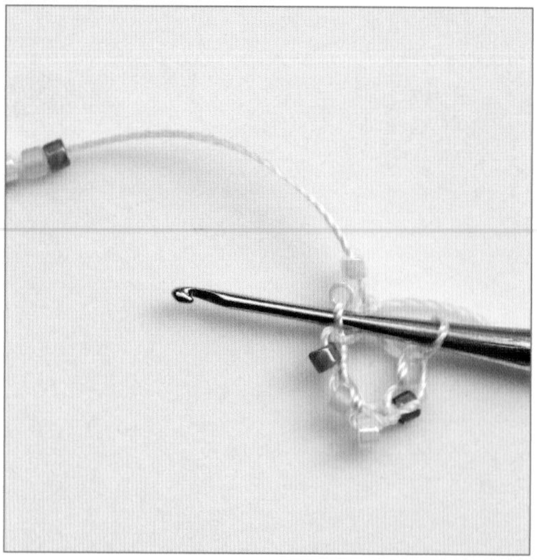

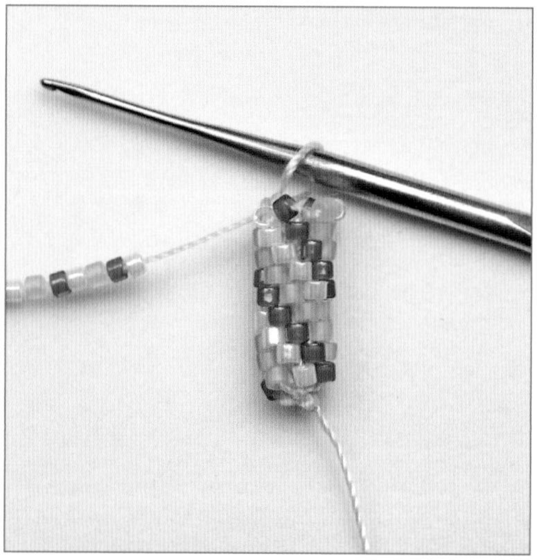

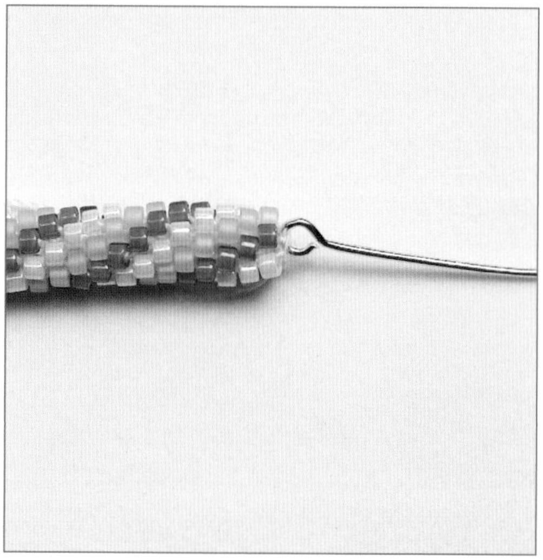

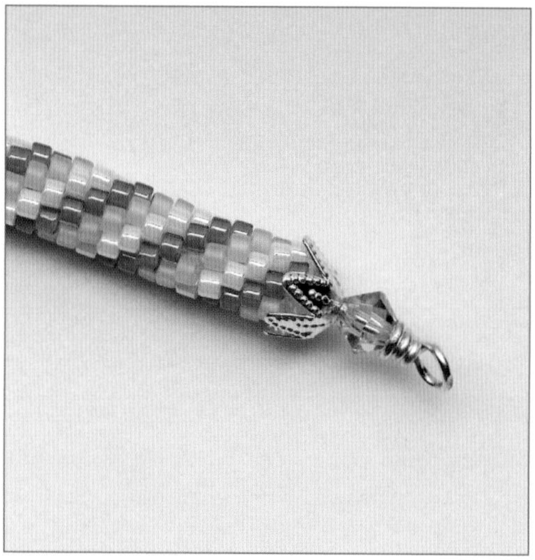

Step 10. Repeat all steps to make your second tube but use a pattern consisting of one silver, one white, and one green. You need about 111 inches of beads to get a final product of about 18 and half inches. On the ends of the second tube, attach a headpin and add 3 Swarovski crystals to each end.

Step 11. Attach each tube end to the clasp.

Step 12. Now you need to attach the flower with the bug onto the tubes, and your necklace is complete!

Project 2.

"Black Shell" Necklace

Laurie Nessel & Irina Serbina

Techniques: *glass bead, macramé*

Photo by Gleb Serbin, gserbin.smugmug.co

Black Shell. Fusing Beads

Laurie Nessel

This two-holed bead is actually two beads that have been fused together in the torch. You need to plan ahead where the beads will merge so they will be oriented correctly when they are fused. You can buy 2-holed mandrels but they are limited in size and spacing between holes. By merging two separate beads, you can use any sized mandrel and space them however you like.

Materials and Tools

- Black Shell Bead (two holes)
- 1 rod ivory
- 1 rod clear
- 1 silver leaf
- Black shards: Some people are making and selling shards, and Bullseye sells shards, called confetti. You can make your own shards by coiling glass off the end of a stainless steel tube and blowing it out into a large, thin bubble. Wrap the bubble in a towel and smash it will a hammer. You can vary the shards by mixing colors, burnishing it with silver, adding enamels, etc. Have fun. The possibilities are endless.
- 2 mandrels, whatever size you need
- Graphite paddle

Step 1. Wrap ivory glass around a mandrel and shape into a taper like a football. Heat and roll over 1/2 page of silver leaf. Burnish and melt in silver. Press parallel ridges into the front of the bead using a razor tool. Case with clear. Heat and let the bead flow to stretch the ridges. Shape into a lentil with a graphite paddle or a lentil press. It is okay if the bead doesn't fill the press entirely. Garage in annealing kiln, preferably at 1100F.

Step 2. Repeat Step 1 on the second mandrel. Immediately after garaging it, take the first bead out of the kiln. Be careful; the mandrel will be hot. Quickly cool the mandrel by dunking it in cold water or wiping it with a damp sponge or towel. While holding the first bead, remove the second bead from the kiln. (This is a good time to turn your kiln down to the correct annealing temperature.) Reheat both beads at once by waving them in and out of the far reaches of the flame. Gradually bring them closer to the torch, concentrating the heat where they will connect.

The mandrels should be perpendicular to you and the sections to be fused together should face each other. When those sections are molten, merge the two beads together. Pull them slightly apart to smooth out the bulge created from pressing them together. Before it chills, align the mandrels so they are parallel unless you need them to be at another angle. Infuse heat into the entire bead. Wrap the back of the bead with black shards. Let some of the shards curve around the edges to the front. I like to keep my shards raised but you can melt them flush if you like. Heat the bead evenly and place in the annealer, this time at the regular annealing temperature.

Black Shell. Macramé

Irina Serbina

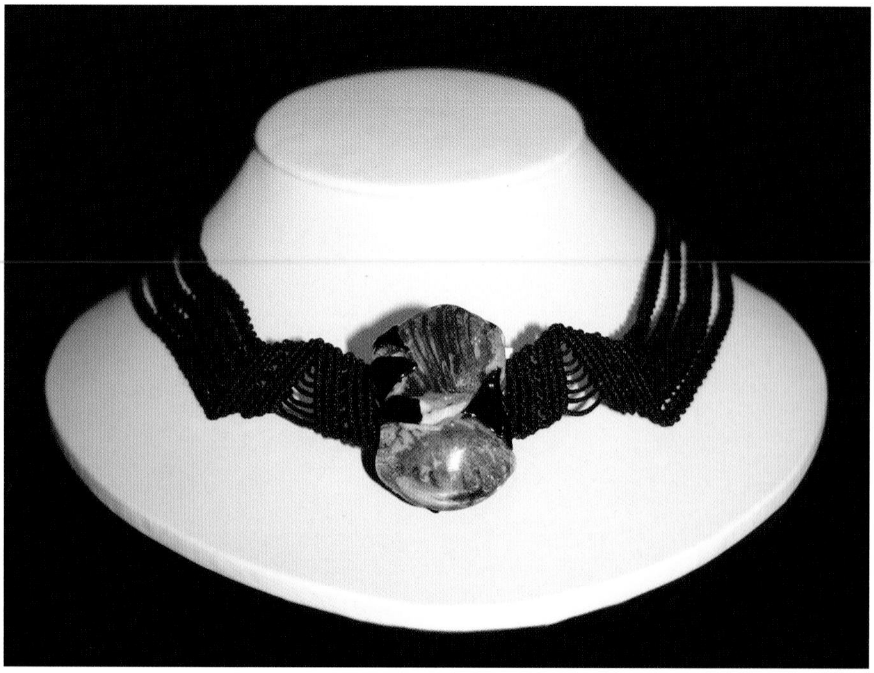

Materials and Tools

- Scissors.
- Working surface. (Firm surface, on which your work can be pinned. Poly-foam, cork or polyurethane will work.
- Long straight pins (T-pins work great)
- 12″ piece of a heavy Soft Flex or Beadalon, to help you get your knotting cord through the hole of some beads.
- Ten pieces of 10ft of Chinese knotting cord.
- Clasp of your choice.

Instructions

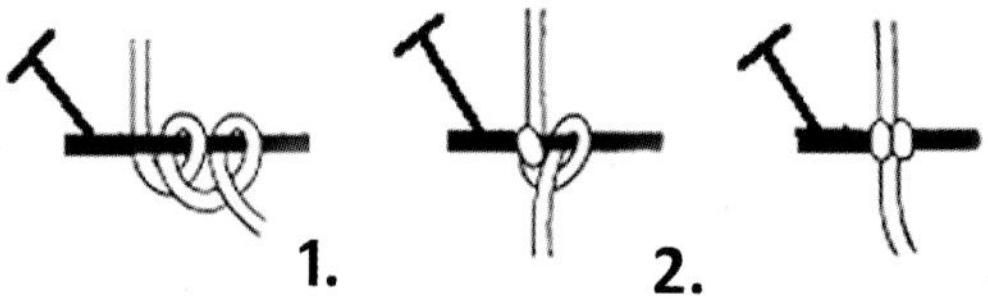

1. 2. 3.

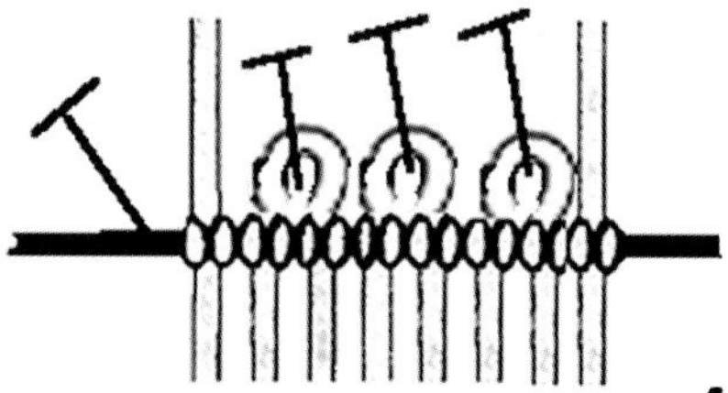

4.

Step 1. Start your necklace by making a line of 8 Horizontal Clove Hitch Knots as shown on the diagram. Cords 1 and 5, which will go through the bead, are tied to the anchor cord exactly in their middles. Cords 2, 3 and 4 are folded in half and pinned down in the middle just above the anchor cord. Both ends of these five cords become "working cords"

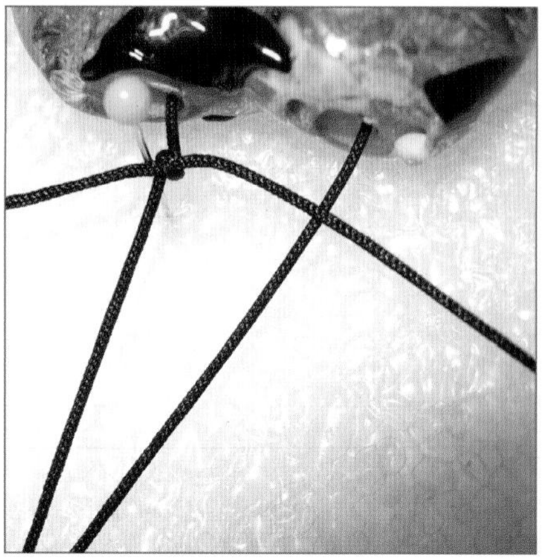

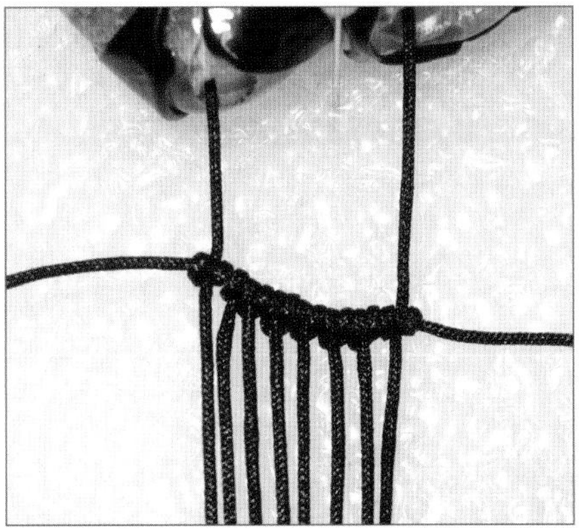

Step 2. Progress.

Step 3. Repeat Step 1 on the other side of the bead, making sure cords 1 and 5 are tied close enough to the bead to hold it tightly between the two anchor cords.

Step 4. Place foremost left cord horizontally across all your working cords; it will become your anchor cord. Clove hitch horizontally across the other cords from left to right. Make sure it is tied closely to the top row, and the anchor cord is pulled taut all the time. Using the cord which became first from the left work to the right making a third row of Clove Hitch Knots. Repeat this step with the rest of your cords, until you have all your cords added.

Step 5. Repeat step 4 on the other side, using the RIGHT cord as an anchor and working from right to left. Make 3 rows of Horizontal Clove Hitch Knots. Make sure it is tied closely to the top row, and the anchor cord is pulled taut all the time.

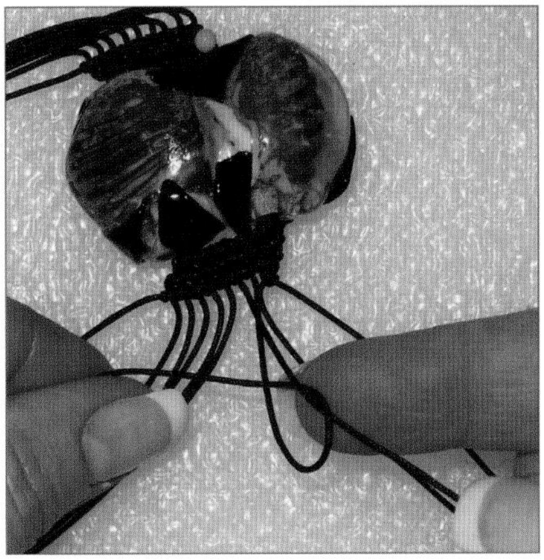

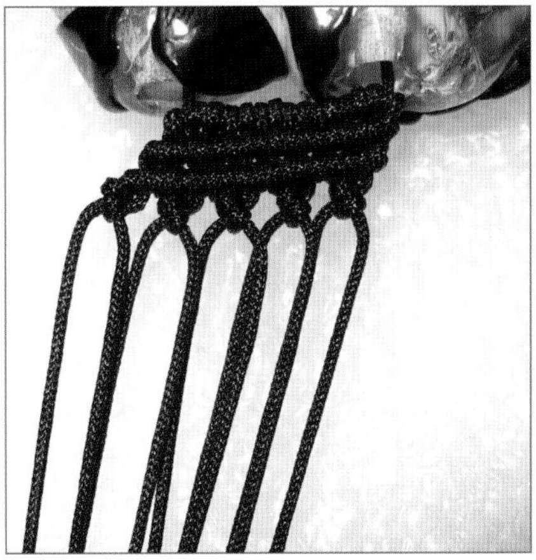

Step 6. Using the second cord from the right as an anchor, and the first cord as a working cord, makes a Vertical Clove Hitch knot. Take cord 4, and use cords 3 for your second Vertical Clove Hitch knot. Repeat on pair of cords working to the left:

- 6 – anchor, 5 – working
- 8 – anchor, 7 – working
- 10 – anchor, 9 – working

Step 7. Make a line of Horizontal Clove Hitch knots using first cord on the right as an anchor. Repeat Step 7 two more times.

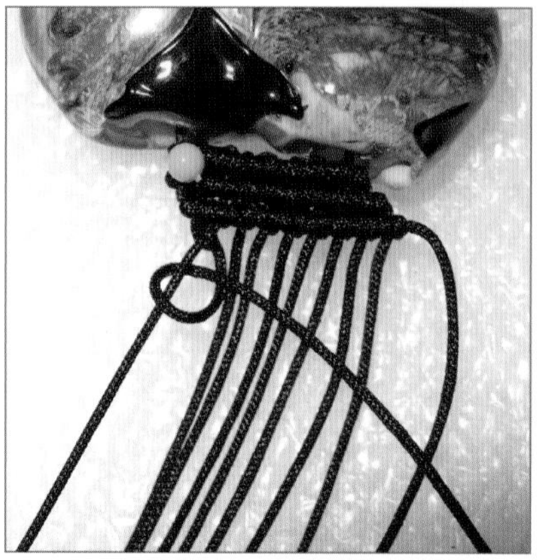

Step 8. Turn your work to pin it down as shown on the picture, repeat steps 4 through 7 on the left side, working from the LEFT to RIGHT.

Below:
Step 9. Repeat steps 4 to 7 again on each side, pulling the anchor cord while making row 8 at a 45 degree angle to the previous row, leaving free hanging cords and changing the direction of your design element. You may want to place a few pins in the board, marking your TARGET ANGLE.

Diagram 1

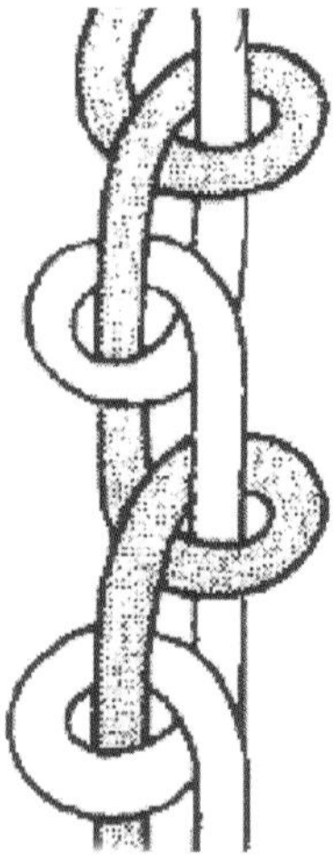

Left and Below:
Step 10. TURN YOUR WORK OVER to have your necklace facing DOWN. Make an 8″ chain of alternating left and right Half Hitch knots on each pair of cords *[see Diagram 1 for an example of alternating left and Right Half Hitch knots]* Turn your work face up again. Make a double line of Horizontal Clove Hitch knots on each side of the necklace to connect all the chains. Work from INSIDE OUT, using inside cord as an anchor.

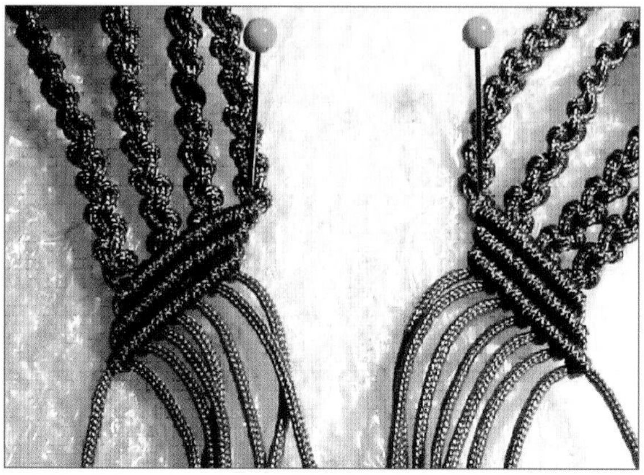

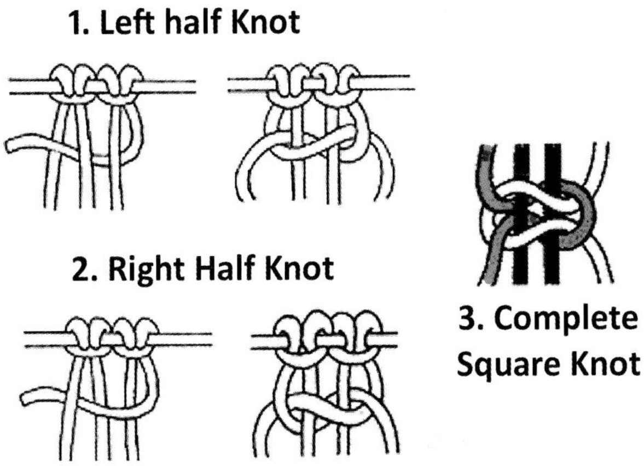

Step 11. Pull two end cords through the clasp in the opposite directions; These will become your WORKING CORDS. Pull two working cords to bring clasp down to 1/2 inch from the last Clove Hitch row. Split all the rest of the cords in half and fold them back around the clasp on each side. All these cords will serve as filler cords for your finishing square knot sinnet. Add two folded cords of CONTRAST color to the "filler cords" bunch, loops down.

Step 12. Make 3-4 square knots with your working cords, working from the top (clasp) down (toward the necklace) as shown on the picture.

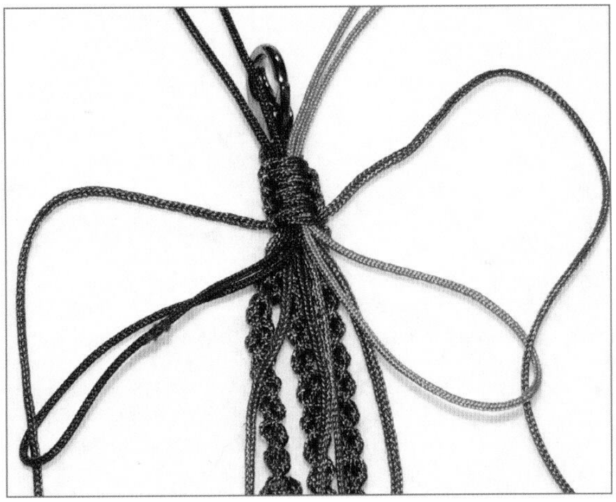

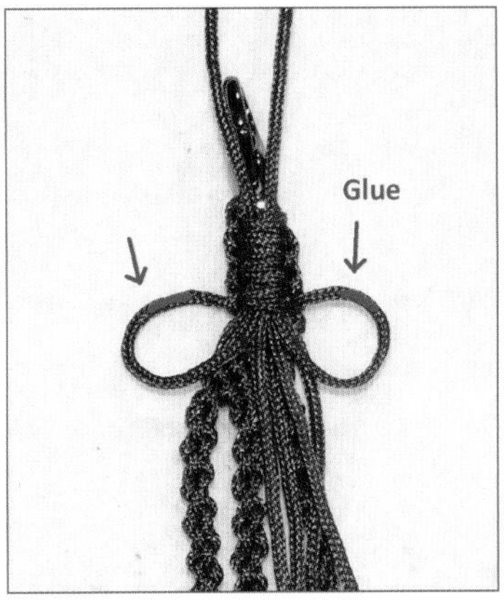

Step 13. Pull your working cord through one of the contrast color loops at the end of the sinnet, pull the looped cord up bringing the end of the working cord inside the sinnet of square knots. DO NOT pull the working cord all the way through – leave 1 inch loop to add glue to the sinnet. Repeat the same with the other working cord.

Step 14. Pull gently on each of the filler cords, to adjust and align them nicely. Add a drop of glue on the part of the working cord, which will be hidden inside the square knot sinnet, and pull cords up all the way.

Step 15. Let the glue set and trim the ends.

This is how a finished clasp should look.

Project 3.

Sexy Choker

Lana May and Albina Manning
Techniques: *wire work, beading stitch—raw*

Materials and Tools

- 17 Czech fire-polished beads, 6mm
- 30 Czech fire-polished beads, 8mm
- 24 Bicone beads, 6mm
- 8 Swarovski pearl beads, 10mm
- 16 Rondelle beads, 6mm
- 24 twisted bugle beads, 6mm
- 14 seed beads, size 11/0
- 20 gr. seed beads, size 6/0
- 14 lb. Fire Line 14lb;
- 2 needles size 10;
- Headpin sp, 21 ga
- Jump ring, sp, 5mm round, 18 gauge
- Clasp, lobster claw, silver-plated brass, 10.6 x7.3x4.3mm
- Chain, silver-plated, 5x3.5mm cable

Instructions

Beading Technique

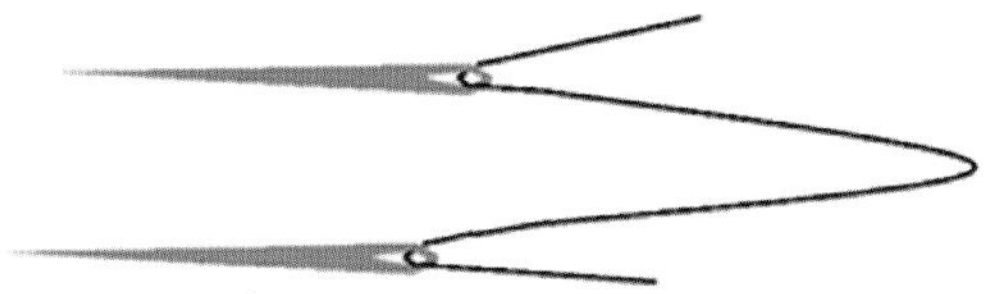

Step 1. Cut the thread length 1-1/2 yard. Use two needles, one on each end of the tread.

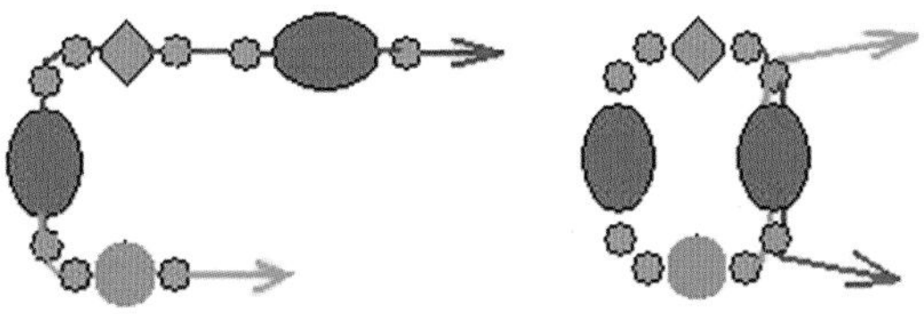

Step 2. String 9 beads: one size 6/0 bead; one 6mm; two size 6/0; one 8mm; two size 6/0, one bicone; and one size 6/0. Slide them to the center of the thread.

Pick up three beads: one size 6/0; one 8mm; and one size 6/0. Pass one needle through from left to right and pass the other needle through from right to left.

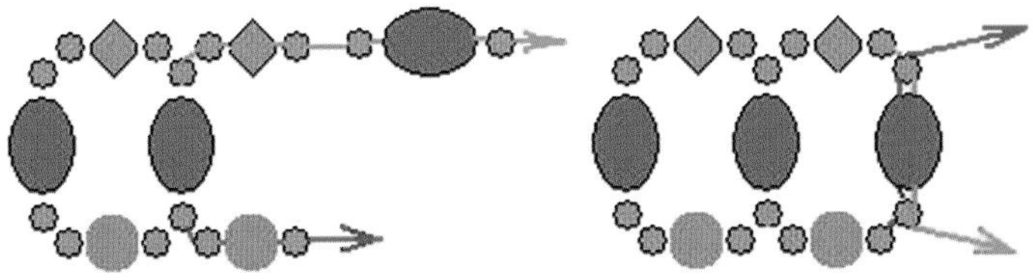

Step 3. On the upper needle: pick up one size 6/0 bead; one bicone; two size 6/0; one 8mm; and one size 6/0 bead.
On the lower needle: pick up one size 6/0 bead, one 6mm, and one size 6/0.

Pass through last 3 beads from upper needle. Repeat Steps 3 and 4 until you have eight 8mm beads *[see step 4]*.

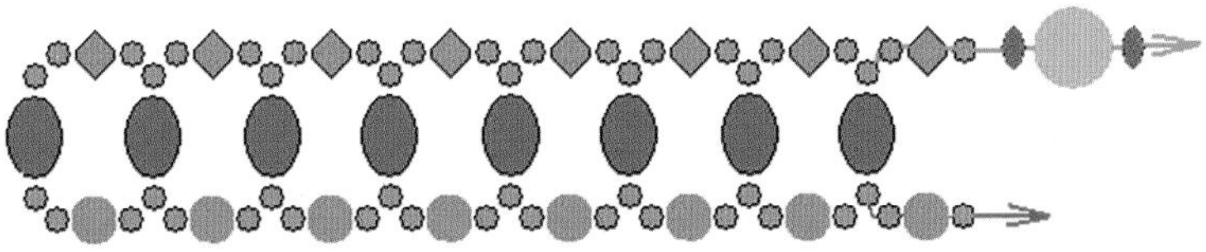

Step 4. Next, on the upper needle, pick up one size 6/0 bead; one bicone; one size 6/0; one rondelle; one 10mm pearl; and one rondelle.
On the lower needle pick up one size 6/0 bead, one 6mm, and one size 6/0 bead.

Pass through last 3 beads from upper needle.

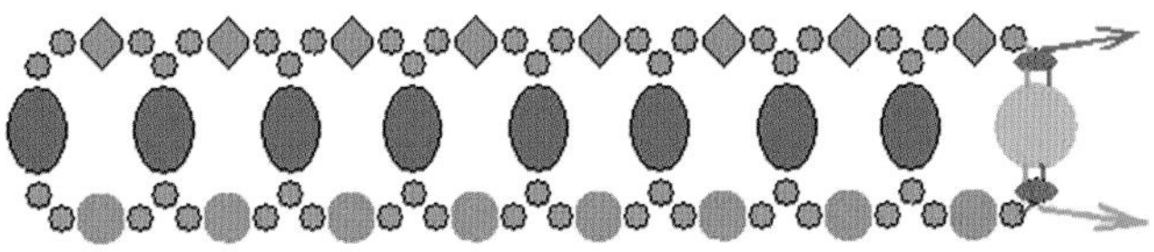

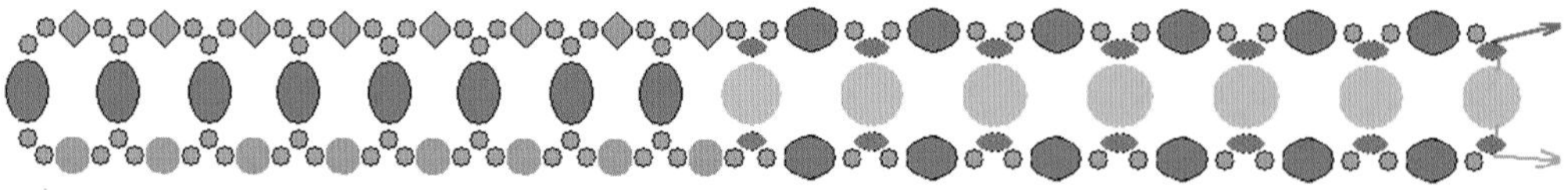

Step 5. On the upper needle pick up one size 6/0 bead; one 8mm; one size 6/0; one rondelle; one 10mm pearl; and one rondelle.
On the lower needle: pick up one size 6/0 bead, 8mm, one size 6/0. Pass through last three beads from upper needle. Repeat last two steps until you have seven 10mm pearls.

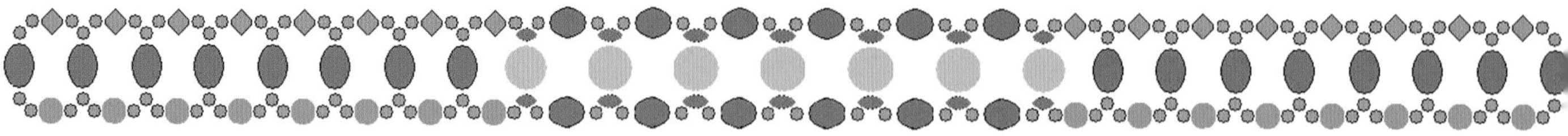

Repeat Steps 2 and 3 until you have eight 8mm beads on the right side necklace.

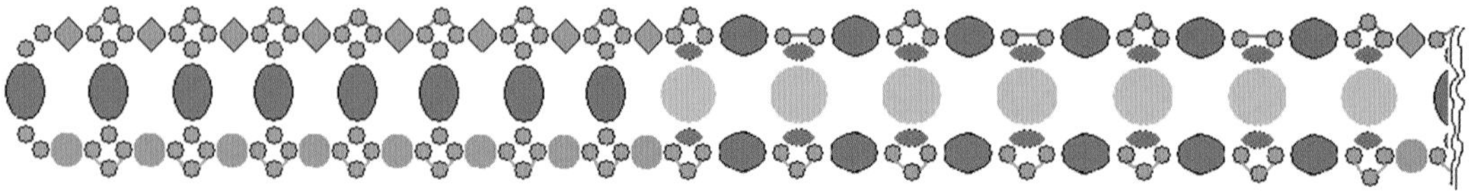

Step 6. Pass through upper and lower part of choker and pick up one size 6/0 bead between every pair of size 6/0 beads, but skip three points on the middle upper part of choker.

Wire Work

Step 7. On a headpin, string one twisted bugle bead; one seed bead 11/0; and one twisted bugle bead.

Make a loop on one end of a headpin. Slide beads to the loop and make another loop close to the bugle. Repeat 11 times to make twelve of these pieces.

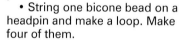

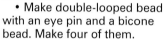

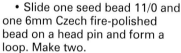

Step 8. Prepare the following pieces:

- String one bicone bead on a headpin and make a loop. Make four of them.
- Make double-looped bead with an eye pin and a bicone bead. Make four of them.
- Slide one seed bead 11/0 and one 6mm Czech fire-polished bead on a head pin and form a loop. Make two.
- On an eye pin, slide one rondelle; one 10mm Swarovski® Pearl; and one rondelle. Make another loop.

Assembling

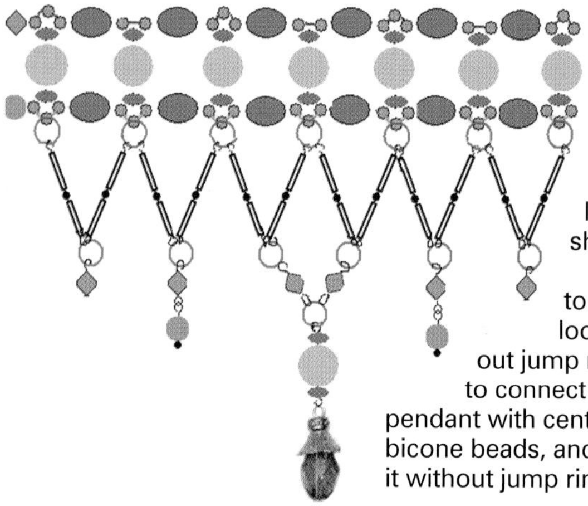

Step 9. Using jump rings (red circles), connect bugle parts *[Step 7]* to the choker's size 6/0 seed beads and with the single and double-looped bicone beads as shown.

Join fire-polished beads to the two outer double-looped bicone beads without jump rings. Use a jump ring to connect the rondelle-Swarovski pendant with center two double-looped bicone beads, and add the capped bead to it without jump rings, as illustrated here.

Clasp

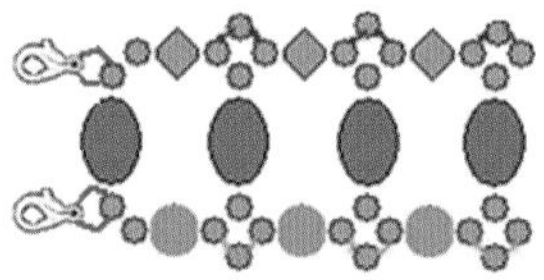

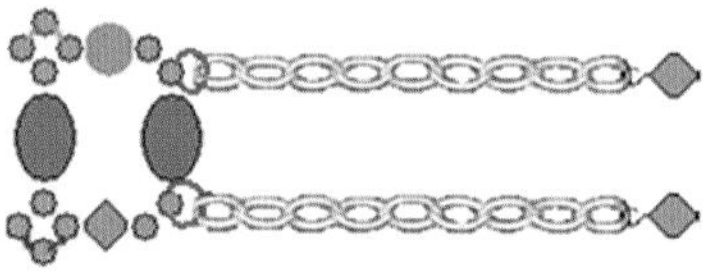

Step 10. Using jump rings, connect lobster claw clasps to the last seed beads in upper and lower parts at one end of the choker. Then, connect two 3" chains on the other end. You can decorate with bicone beads each end of chain.

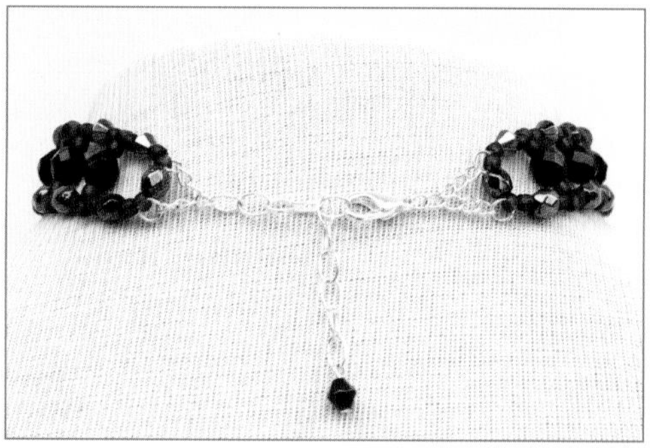

This is a single-chain variation of clasp.

Project 4.

"The Harmony of Three" Necklace

Albina Manning and Geri Cook

Techniques: *wire work, beading stitch*

3-Loop Clasp

Albina Manning

Materials and Tools

- 20ga round dead soft wire – 1 foot
- Round-nose pliers
- Wire cutters
- Flat-nose pliers

Instructions

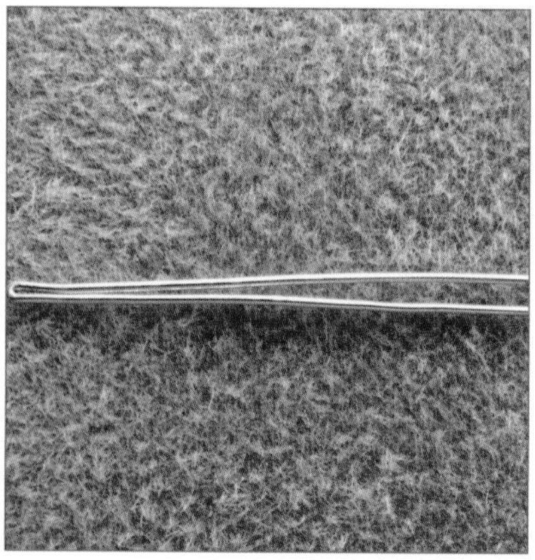

Step 1: Cut the wire 3-1/2" long. Using pliers, fold wire in half.

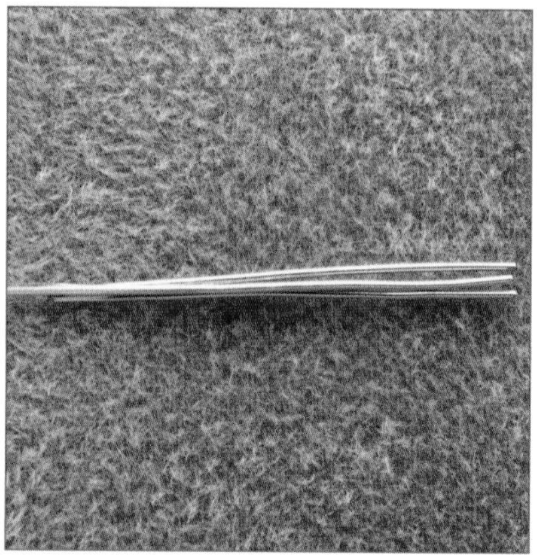

Step 2: Cut another piece of wire 3 1/2" long and place it between two ends of the folded wire so all three ends are even.

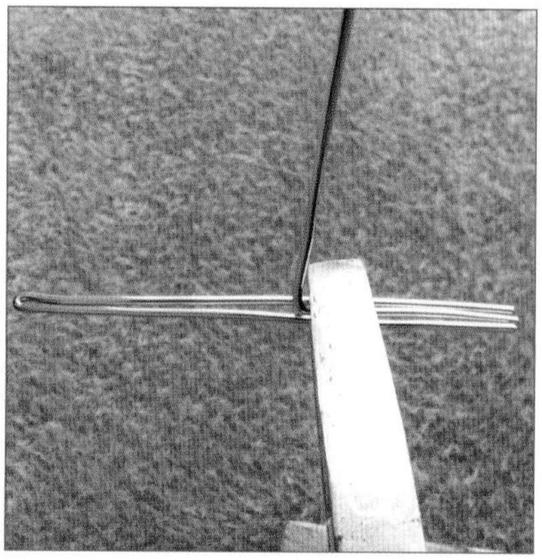

Step 3: Grip all three ends of wire with flat-nose pliers so the distance between the folded end and the pliers is 1 inch (2.5cm). Bend the straight, middle wire to the angle of 90°.

Step 4: Keeping the wire ends close to each other, start wrapping the bent wire around the other two.

Step 5: Make 6 coils and trim the wire so the trimmed end is in the middle. Pinch the trimmed end in the place.

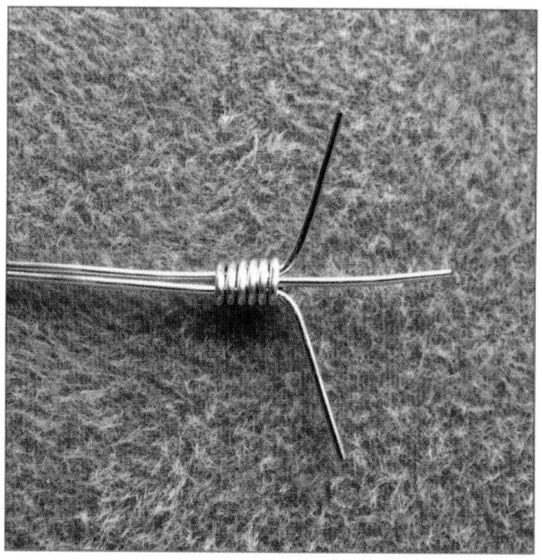

Step 6: Pull two outside wires apart at about a 90° angle.

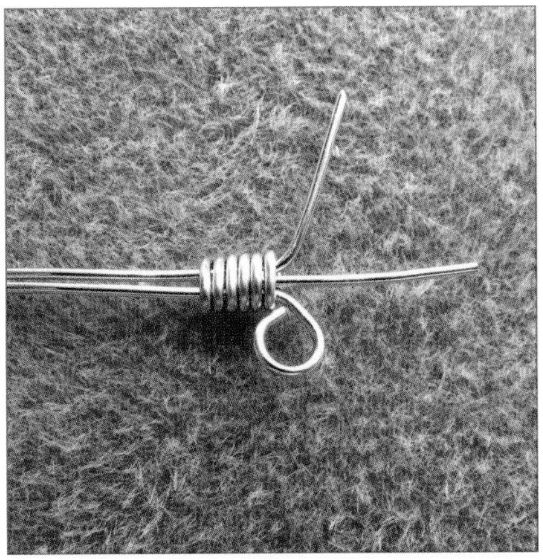

Step 7: Using round-nose pliers, make a simple loop as shown.

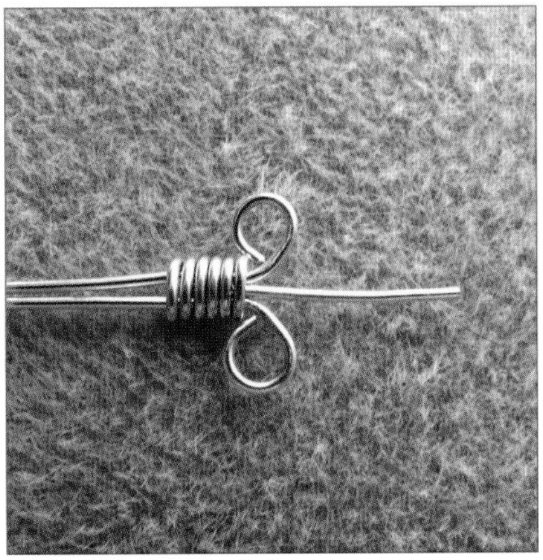

Step 8: Repeat Step 7 with the other outside wire end.

Step 9: Bend the middle wire into a third simple loop.

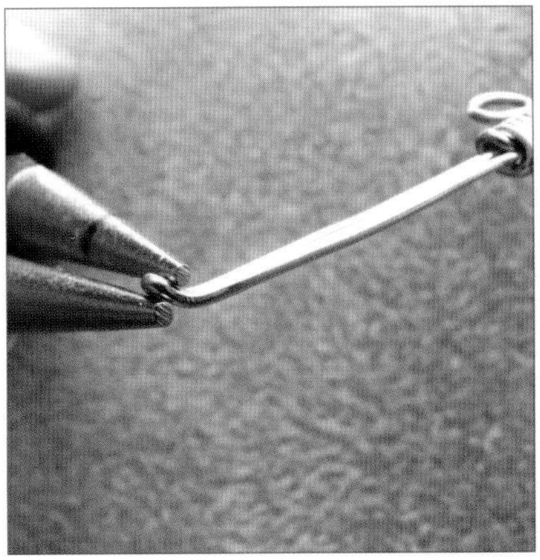

Step 10: Grip the tip of folded end of the wire with the very end of round-nose pliers and bend it to about 45°.

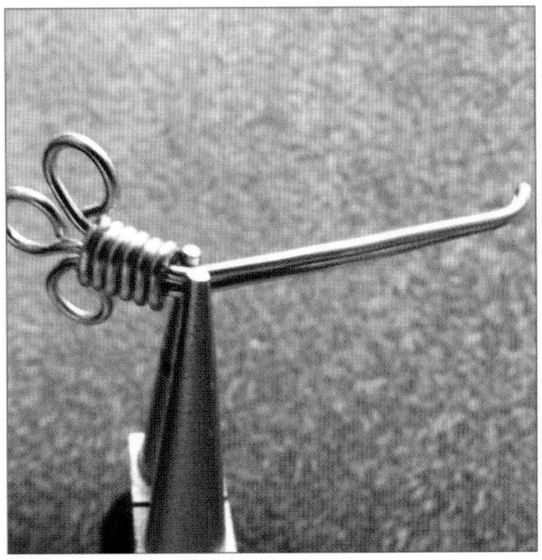

Step 11: Grip the two parallel wires at the base of the coil and bend it at about 45° angle in the same direction as you did in Step 10.

Step 12: Bend the hook in the opposite direction around the thick part of round-nose pliers.

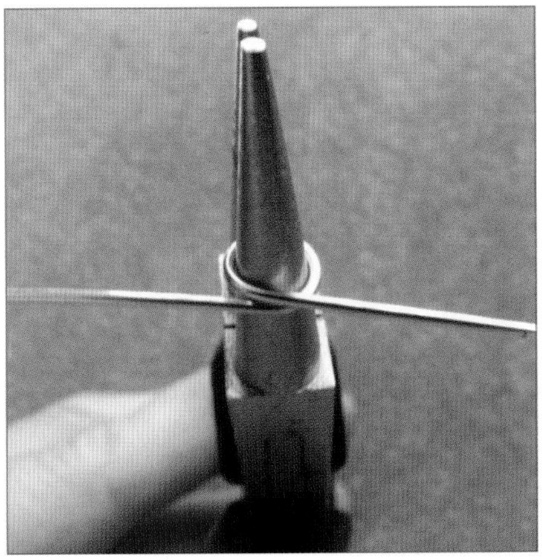

Step 13: Cut a second wire 2" long. Place the wire in the middle of the round-nose pliers and bend into a complete circle with the wire ends forming a straight line.

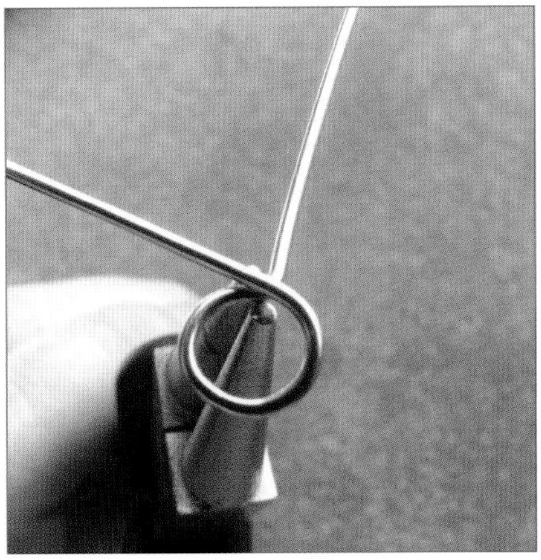

Step 14: Hold one wire with the tip of round-nose pliers and bend it 90°.

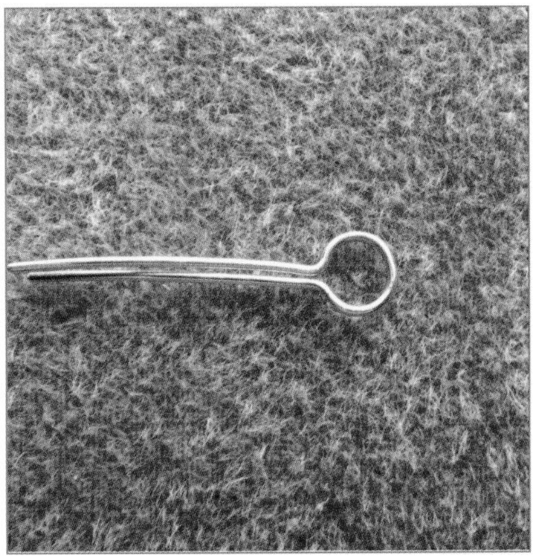

Step 15: Repeat Step 14 with the other end of the wire so the two ends are parallel.

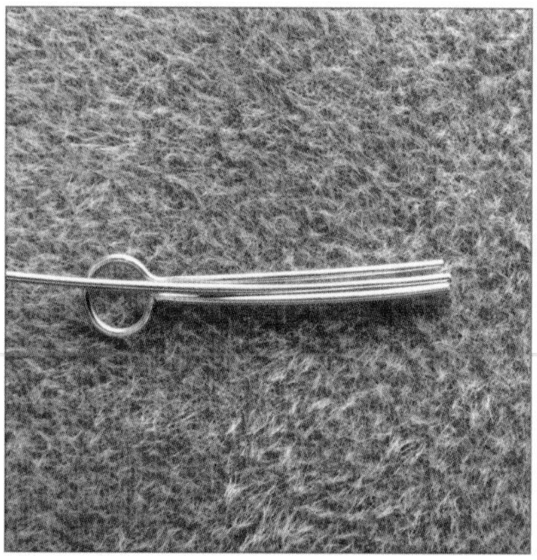

Step 16: Cut a piece of wire 3" long and place it between two sides of the wire so the three ends are even.

Step 17: Grip all three wires with flat-nose pliers at the base of the circle and bend the middle wire to a 90° angle. Keeping the wire ends close to each other, start wrapping like you did in Steps 4 & 5, making six coils and trimming the wrapping wire so the trimmed end is in the middle. Pinch the trimmed end in the place.

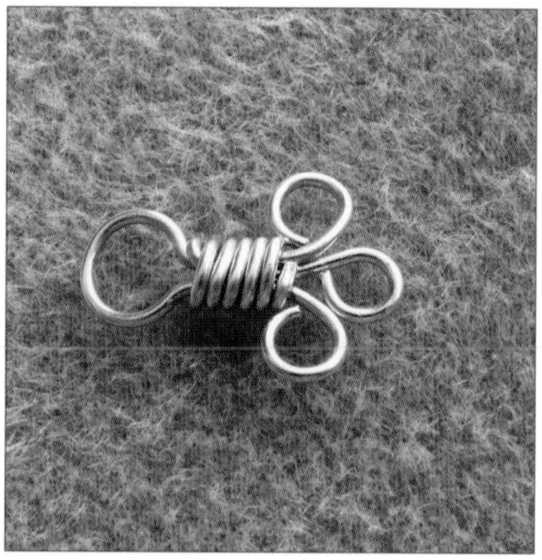

Step 18: Repeat Steps 6-9 to make 3 loops.

Step 19: You can decorate you clasp with beads. Slide one 4mm bead on 22ga headpin and make a wrapped loop. Repeat to make 6 wrapped beads.

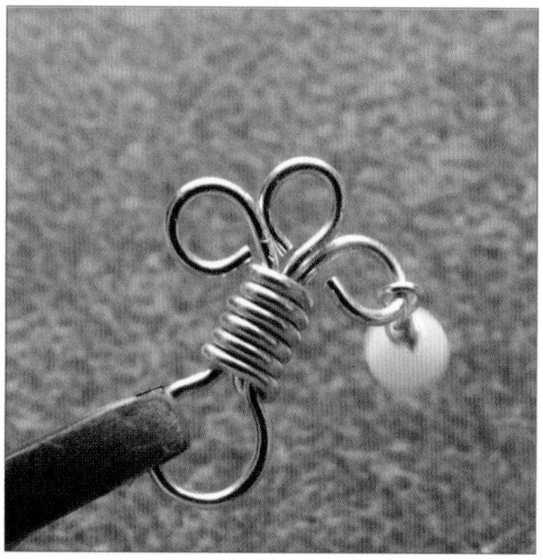

Step 20: Open one loop of a clasp and slide on the wrapped bead. Close the loop.

Step 21: Repeat step 20 with the other loops.

Beading Technique

Geri Cook

When presented with a three-strand clasp created by Albina Manning, I was challenged to come up with a jewelry design that was different than anything I'd previously seen in beading books and magazines. The result was this three-strand necklace that will allow you to showcase your stringing and bead weaving skills. The spiral rope stitch used to showcase the focal bead is easy enough even for a beginner.

Materials and Tools

- 10g size 11/0 beads in a solid color (A)
- 20g size 11/0 seed bead mix (B)
- 5g size 8/0 seed bead mix (C)
- 10 6mm Swarovski crystals
- Focal bead
- Beading wire
- Crimp beads & crimping tool
- Fire line or Wildfire beading thread
- Wire cutters
- Crimping tool
- Scissors
- Size 10 beading needle

Instructions

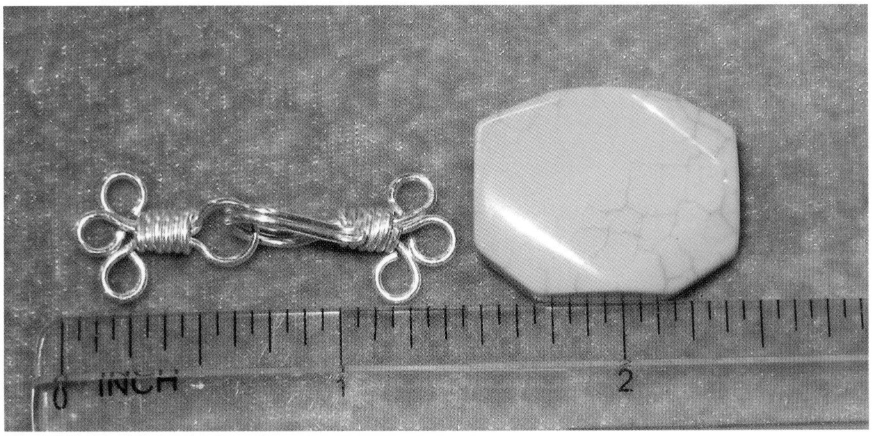

Step 1: Determine the length desired for the shortest strand. Add an additional inch or more to this length for the second strand, and then one to two additional inches to this length for the third strand.

Step 2: Measure the length of your clasp and focal bead. Subtract this amount from the total length of the third strand. Divide the resulting amount by 2. This is the amount you will need to stitch on both sides of the focal bead.

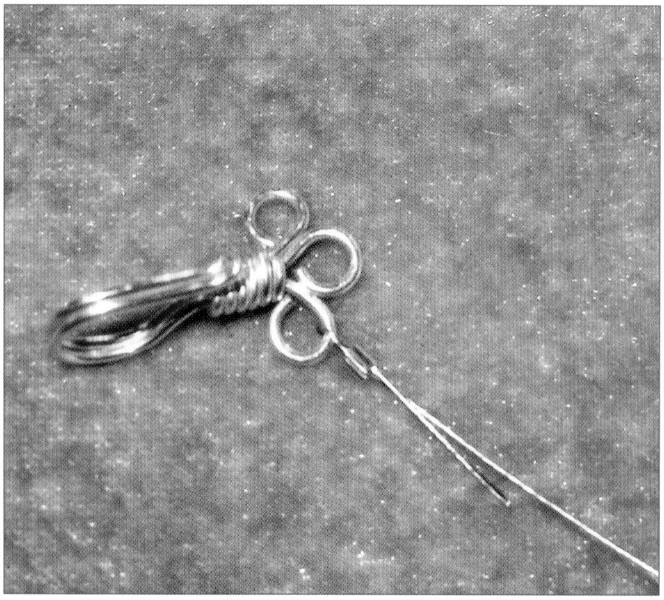

Step 3: For the first strand of the necklace, cut a length of beading wire at least 3" longer than your desired length. String a crimp bead and run the wire through the one loop of the clasp. Double back through the crimp bead and crimp the beading wire using the crimping tool. String the 11/0 seed bead mix the desired length and attach to other part of clasp.

Step 4: Repeat Step 3 using the 8/0 seed bead mix for the second strand, incorporating the crystals.

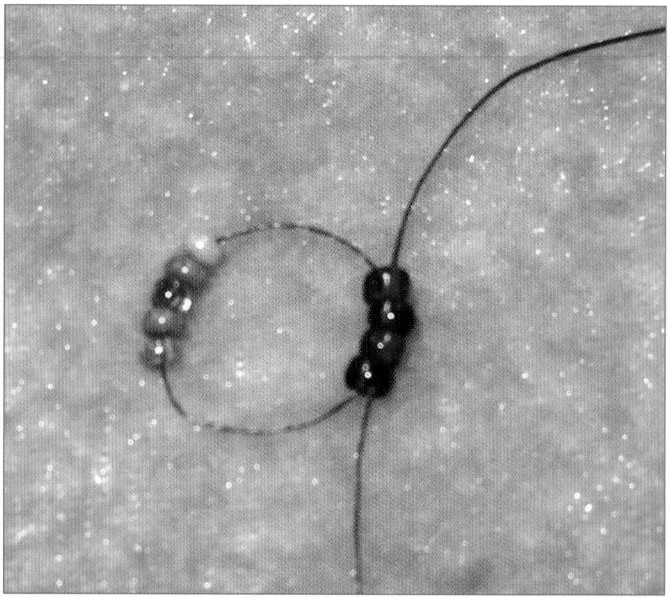

Step 5: To start the first side of the third strand, thread a needle with 6' of thread. String 4 A beads and 5 B beads. Slide the beads to within 12" of the end of the thread. (The 12" of thread will be used to attach the necklace to one end of the clasp.) Insert the needle UP through the 4 A beads to form your first loop (see illustration). Insert the needle DOWN through the 5 B beads. Now insert your needle UP through the 4 A beads once more. This will lock the starting beads in place.

Step 6: If you are right-handed, hold the beads between your thumb and pointer finger with the 5 B beads to your left. Left-handers hold the beads with the 5 B beads to their right. Keep the thread tail pointing toward the floor.

Step 7: Pick up 1 A bead and 5 B beads. Slide the beads past your needle. Count back 3 A beads of the previous loop and insert your needle UP through these three beads. Pull up the excess thread so that the newly added beads meet the work. Flip this new loop of beads to your left UNDERNEATH your first loop. Insert your needle UP through the new A bead. LH: Flip the loop to your right ON TOP OF the previous loop. Repeat this step until you reach the point where the focal bead is to be added. Add in a new working thread when needed.

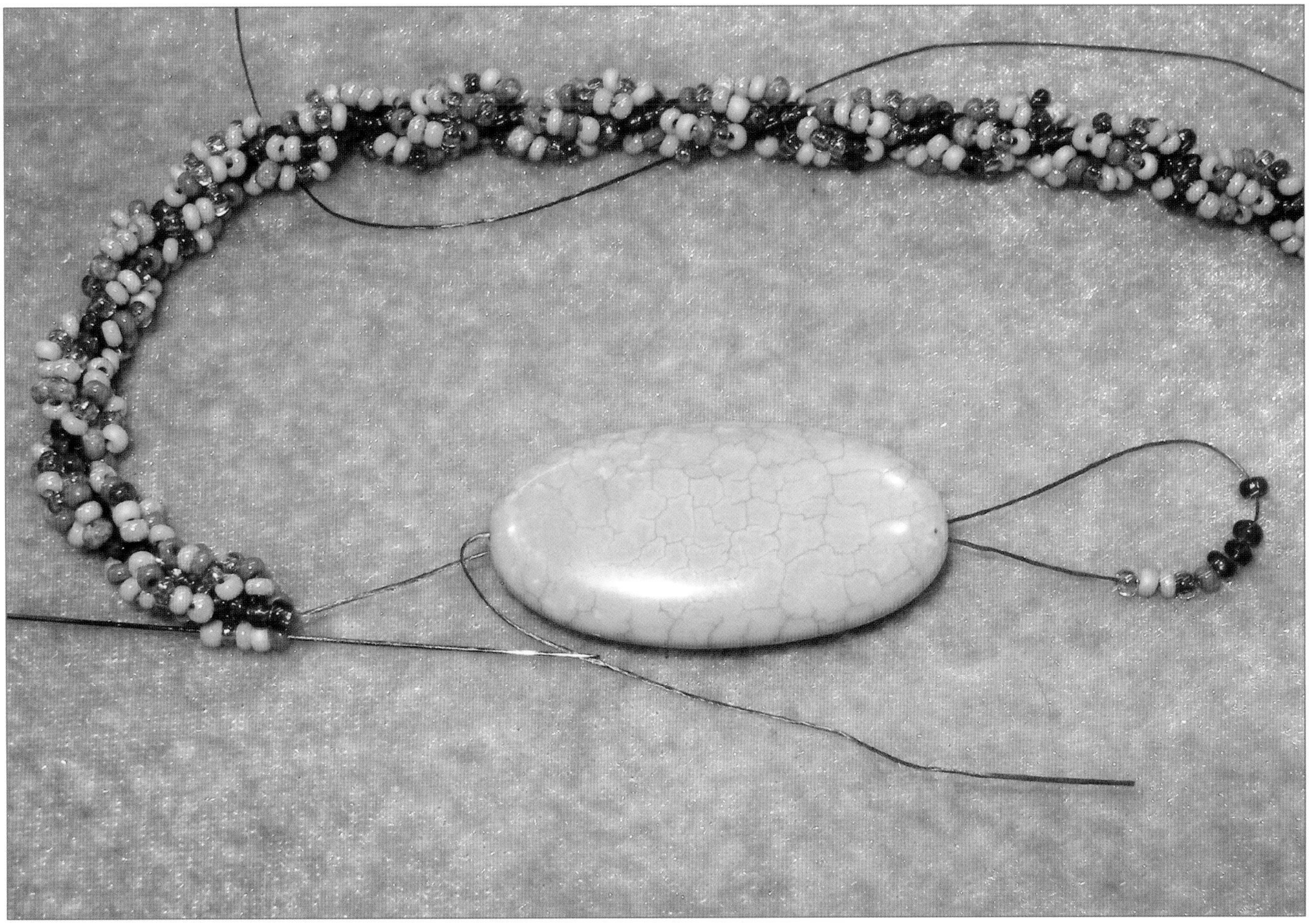

Step 8: To attach the focal bead: After making the last loop of the first half, string your focal bead, 4 A beads and 5 B beads. Insert your needle DOWN through the focal bead and the 5 B beads of your last loop (see illustration). Pull up the excess thread.

Step 9: Insert your needle UP through the 4 A beads to which the loop is attached and the focal bead. Pull up tightly.

Step 10: Insert your needle UP through the 4 new A beads and then DOWN through the 5 new B beads, the focal bead and the 5B of the last loop. Pull up tightly.

Step 11: Insert your needle UP through the 4 A beads and the focal bead. Pull up tightly. Insert your needle UP through the 4 A beads. Weave the second half the same as the first half.

Step 12: To attach the clasp: Pick up 7 B beads and the clasp. Insert your needle through the opposite side of the A bead from which your thread is exiting. Weave through this loop of beads at least three times to secure the bead work to the clasp.

Step 13: Once you feel the work is secure, weave back down through the necklace following your thread path to secure the working thread. Tie a half-hitch knot when done and snip the working thread. Use the 12" tail to attach the opposite end of the necklace.

Project **5.**

Warm and Cool Earrings

Albina Manning and Olena Bugrimenko

Techniques: *wire work, chain maille*

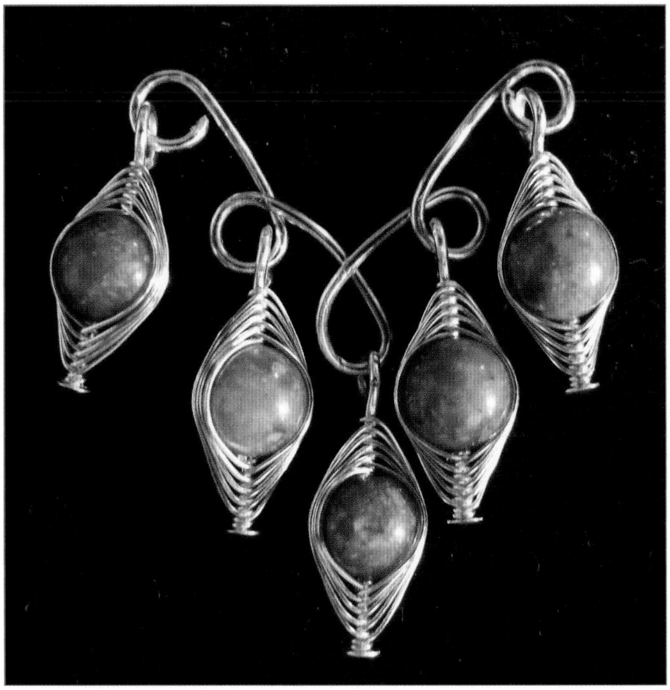

Herringbone Beads

Albina Manning

Materials and Tools

- Wire 22ga
- Headpin 22 ga
- Beads 10mm
- Jump rings 5mm 18ga
- Pliers
- Jump ring tool

Instructions

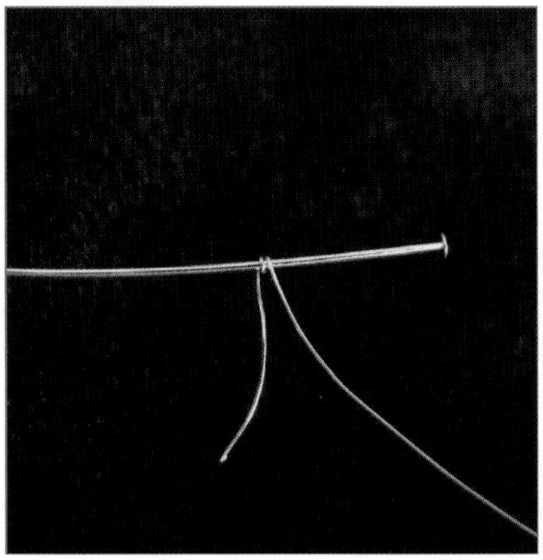

Step 1: Attach 28 ga wire to the 22 ga headpin by coiling twice, so the short tale is towards to the open end. Trim the short tail.

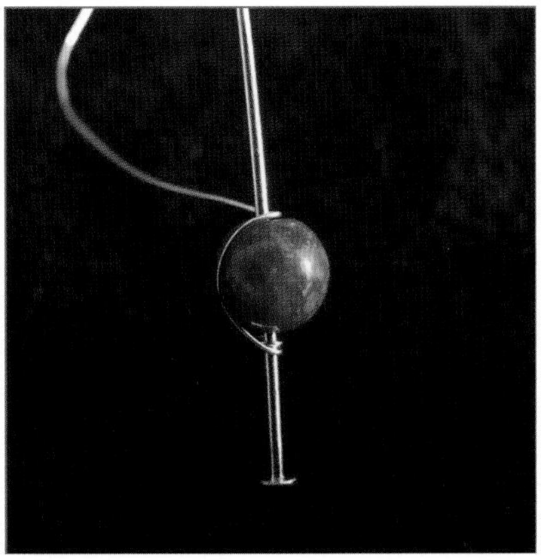

Step 2: Slide a bead on the headpin. Take the wire to the other side of the bead and loop once. Always loop over the headpin.

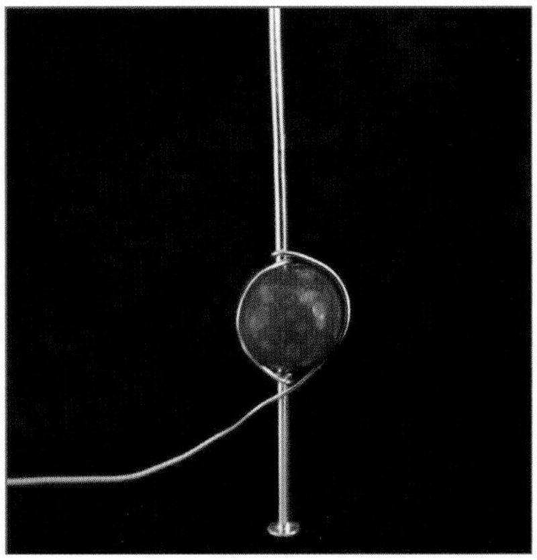

Step 3: Take the wire to opposite side and wrap it over the headpin again. Now, you have one complete frame around the bead.

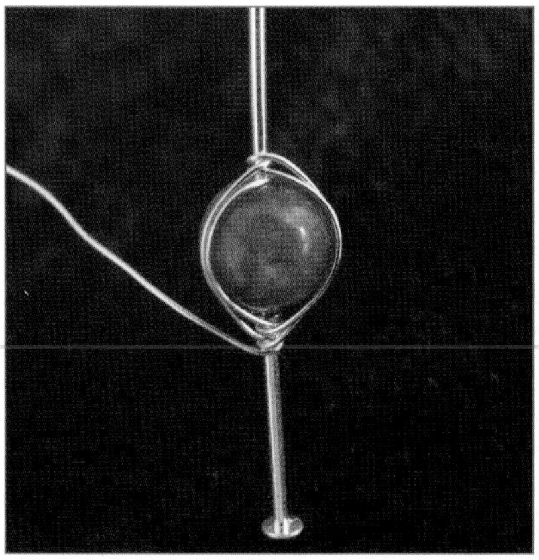

Step 4: Take the wire down and up again in the same manner looping the wire over the headpin so you have the second frame. Notice that you place the wire behind the previous wire frame.

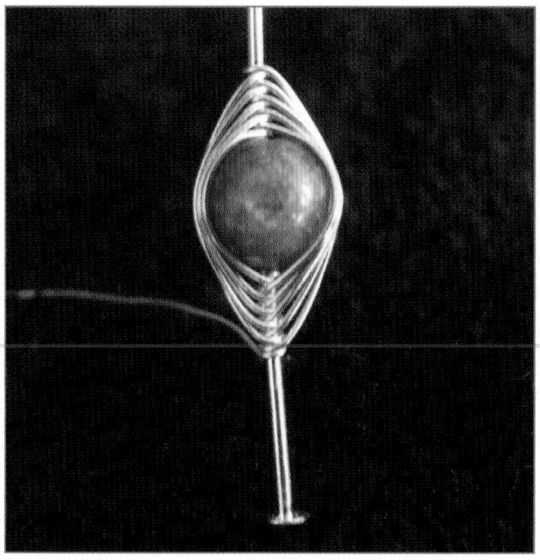

Step 5: Repeat Step 4 until you have 5 frames around the bead. When you finish wrapping, secure the wire by coiling 1-1/2 times around the headpin. Trim very close on the back of the bead, and then press in the cut end with chain-nose pliers.

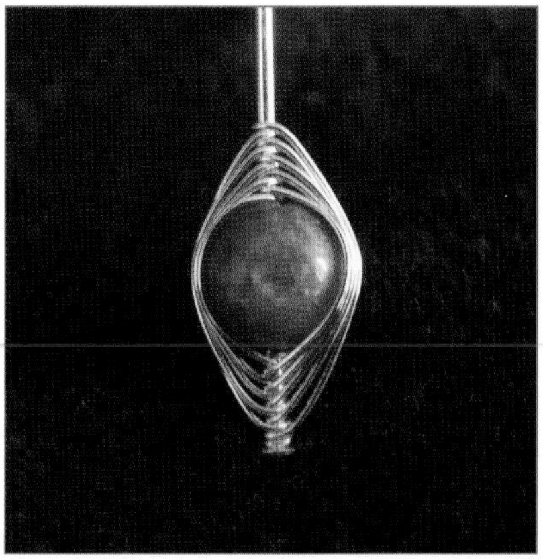

Step 6: Gently slide the bead towards the head of headpin. You may want to use chain-nose pliers to hold headpin.

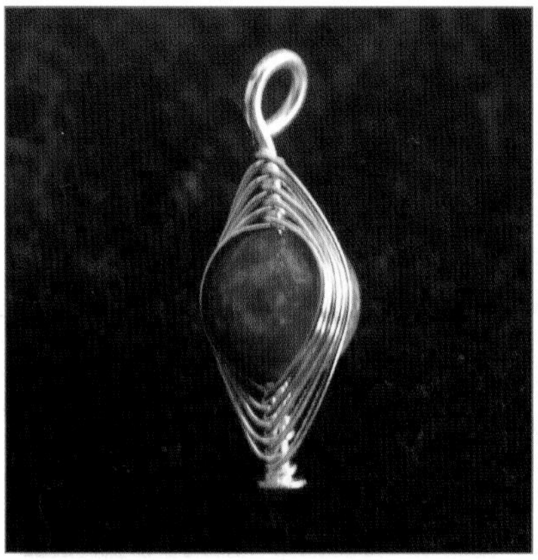

Step 7: Using your chain-nose pliers, bend the wire to form a right angle as close to the bead as possible. Make simple loop using round-nose pliers. Make 5 beads.

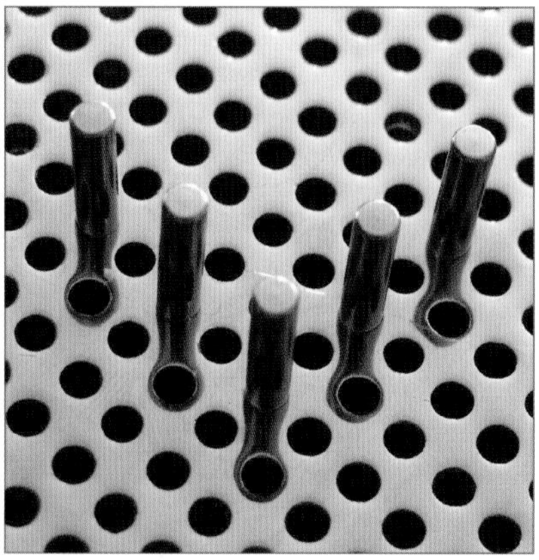

Step 8: Position the pegs in your jig using the 45 degree angle.

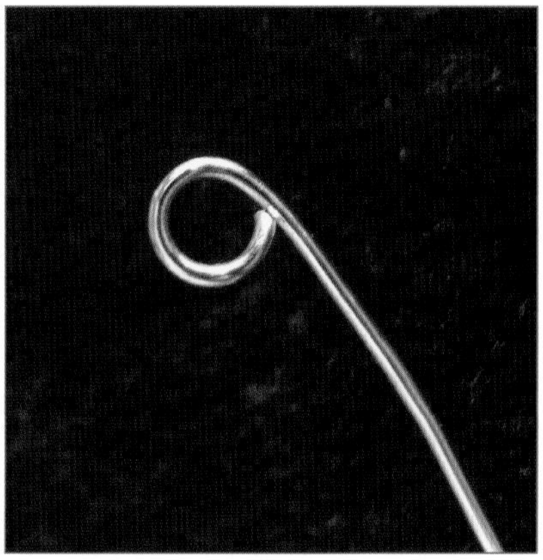

Step 9: Make a loop in one end of the wire.

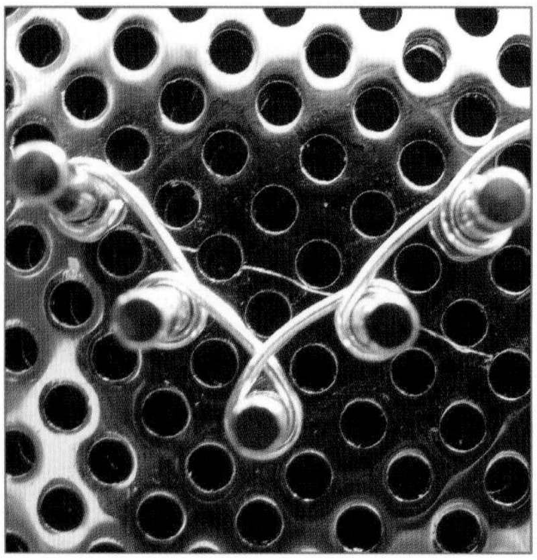

Step 10: Place the loop wire on one of the end pegs in the pattern and wrap the wire as shown.

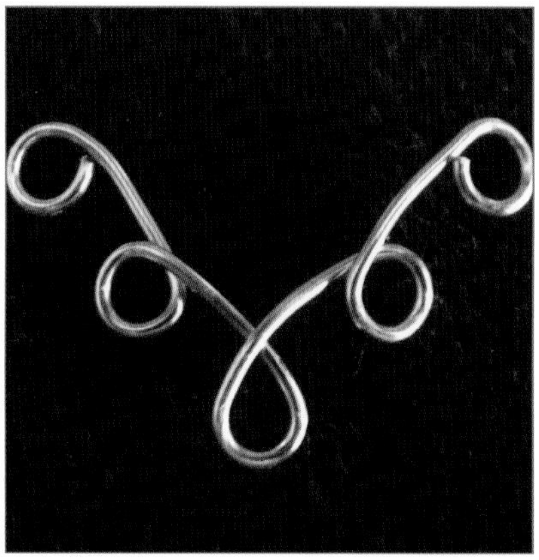

Step 11: Remove the wire from the jig and cut the excess wire at the end with your flush cutter. Close the final loop using your chain-nose pliers.

Step 12: Attach a herringbone wrapped bead to each loop.

Chain Maille

Olena Bugrimenko

Step 1. Make a 2-2-2 chain of jump rings. Pick up an open ring and slip 4 closed rings into it. Close the open ring. Pass a second open ring through the 4 closed rings, and close it.

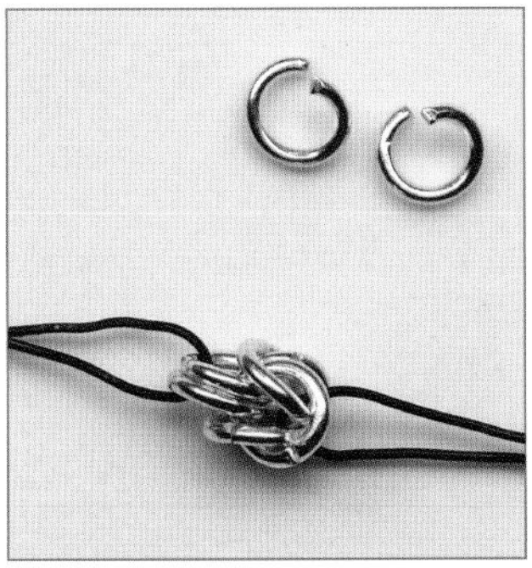

Step 2. Hold the 2 closed rings that are on the left side. Move the 2 closed rings on the right in opposite directions around the middle rings, so they rest against the rings on the left. For the next step, open 2 rings.

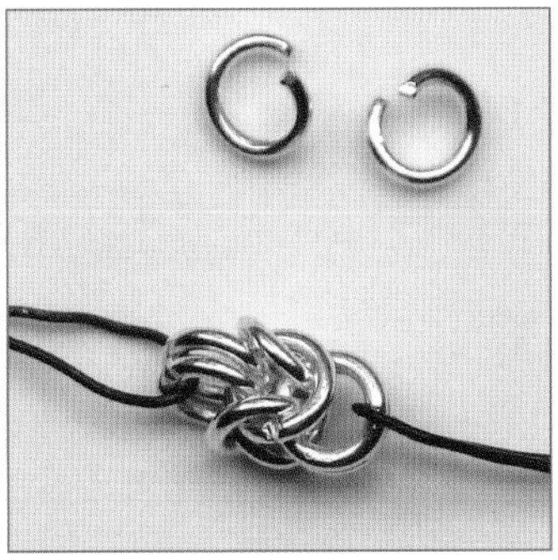

Step 3. Insert the two open rings, between the two original middle rings and through the two rings that are resting against the left rings. Open 2 more rings.

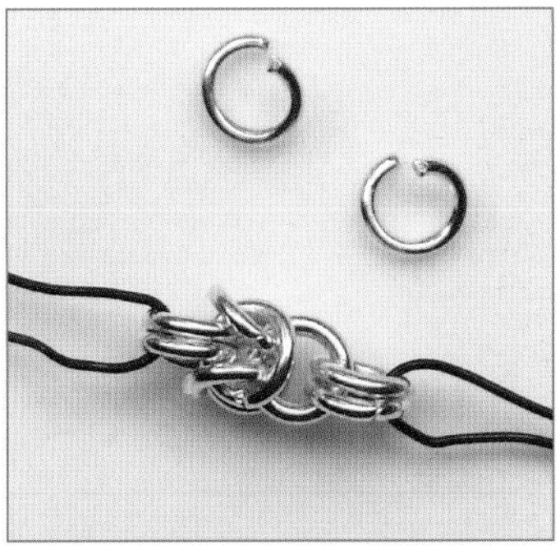

Step 4. Add the two open rings to the two you just added. Open 2 more rings.

Step 5. Add the two additional rings to those you just added.

Step 6. To make the right side look like the left, turn the end rings back toward the middle and grab them between the two rings that were on their left.

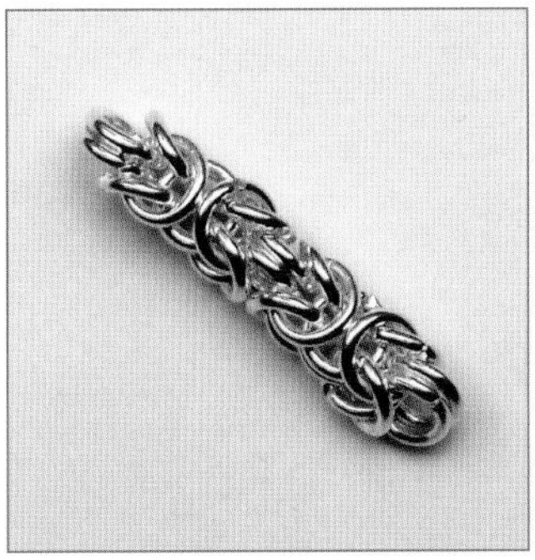

Step 7. Now, repeat steps 2-6 to make it look like the picture.

Step 8. Since you need two of these, you need to follow Steps 1-7 once more.

Step 9. Attach the two chains with the beads and the ear wire. Now, you have one complete earring. To make the second earring, repeat all the steps!

The result.

Project 6.

Beaded Elegance & Clay

Meredith Arnold and Lana May

Techniques: *metal clay & polymer clay, beading netting stitch*

Sometimes a design needs a customized piece to bring it all together. This simple focal point made from metal clay and polymer clay also works as a clasp for the tube netting to create a finished look.

Metal Clay Basics

Metal clays use water to keep them workable. Knowing when the clay is too wet or dry is the key to working successfully with this material. Metal clay that is too dry cracks a lot. Clay that is too wet is like working with toothpaste. At either extreme the clay is difficult to use. Metal clay dries out if left out of the package for any length of time so keep this in mind when working with it.

Metal clays shrink when fired. Different brands and versions have different shrinkage rates. The type used in this project, PMC3, shrinks 10-12%.

Playing cards are used to roll out uniform sheets of clay. Stack two equal piles of cards to roll over, putting the clay between the cards on a Teflon sheet. Roll over the stacks of cards, turning the Teflon sheet as needed to get the size sheet desired for your project.

Metal clay needs to be fired to become fine silver. This is called sintering. All metal clay pieces must be completely dry before firing to avoid creating a steam effect which can blow your pieces apart. Speed up drying using a warming plate or candle warmer for about 5 minutes to insure that all the water has evaporated from a piece.

Finishing the work before firing is much simpler than working with it in the metal form after firing. A simple way to sand rough edges, round corners, or create a beaded (rounded) edge is to use a damp baby wipe and rub gently on the area that needs attention. This also works to create smooth, flat areas on the back of a piece. The metal clay in the used baby wipes can be recycled. Rio Grande Jewelry Supply will take the wipes and recycle the silver from them and give you a credit for what you've sent to them, which will help to keep your costs down and to work "green" at the same time.

Firing can be done in a variety of ways, including the use of a butane torch like that used to make Crème Brulee, a propane Speedfire Cone (like a modified camp stove), a butane Speedfire mini (like a fancy cigar lighter), a gas stove, or a kiln. A kiln is desirable for firing synthetic stones or glass with the metal clay, but all of the other firing methods work well for pieces that are metal clay only.

Metal clay only pieces can be cold quenched after firing to cool them down quickly. Cold quenching is the process of putting the fired pieces into a bowl of water. Use tongs to move the piece to the water. As soon as it hits the water there will be a hissing or a pop sound which means the heat is dissipating; it will be safe to handle after that. Only cold quench pieces that are pure metal clay and don't include glass or stones. The glass or stones will shatter from the extreme temperature change. Pieces with glass or stone inclusions need to cool slowly in the kiln, usually at least two hours, until they are below 200 degrees. Never pick up a metal clay piece that has just been fired. The temperatures reached when firing metal clay can be considered "volcano hot."

Metal Clay Diamond

Meredith Arnold

Materials and Tools

- PMC3, 9 gm. pkg.
- 10 playing cards (two stacks of 5 cards each)
- Roller
- Teflon sheet
- Cutting pin, fine needle or bead piercing pin
- Two sizes of drinking straws

Instructions

Step 1. Roll out a uniform sheet of metal clay and use the pin to cut a diamond shape approximately 2" long and 1-3/4" wide using the pin.

Step 2. Texture the surface by gently pushing the larger drinking straw in a random pattern. Be careful not to push all the way through the clay. Use the smaller straw to make circles inside larger straw circles.

Step 3. Dry the piece thoroughly on a candle warmer or warming plate...not a hot plate.

Step 4. Pre-finish by sanding with a damp baby wipe to finish the edges, smooth surfaces, etc.

Step 5. Fire at 1290° for 10 minutes or so.

Step 6. Cold quench the piece in cold water. Dry the piece and brush gently with a wire brush to get into the low spots of the texture only.

Step 7. Tumble in a tumbler with mixed stainless steel shot and a few drops of dishwashing liquid soap or hand polish the PMC. To hand polish use progressive grit polishing papers from coarsest grit (800) to finest grit (8000) until smooth and shiny.

Polymer Clay Basics

Polymer clay works like pottery clay but comes in many colors. An oil- based solvent is used to make the clay pliable and most clay brands are cured at regular oven temperatures, around 275°. Polymer clay doesn't really dry out when left out on a table. Eventually the solvent will evaporate, a matter of weeks or months, which will make the clay stiffer, but it can be "re-constituted" using a drop or two of mineral oil to soften it up again.

Pre-finishing before baking is always simpler than waiting until after curing the clay. Smooth surfaces, edges, etc. before baking. Polymer clay can be sanded after baking using progressive grits of wet/dry sandpaper from 600-1200 grit, but always sand with water to keep the dust out of the air. A simple satin finish can be achieved by sanding gently with water and #000 fine steel wool, followed by #0000 fine steel wool. Don't push too hard with the scrubbing or there will be scratches on the clay that look white or like bloom on chocolate. Buff the piece on denim or a soft cotton towel to bring up a soft satin sheen.

Polymer Clay Backing Piece

Materials and Tools

- Polymer clay—(1) 2 oz. block of black
- Pasta machine (or Plexiglas roller and 18 playing cards (to determine thickness)
- Index card
- Teflon sheet
- Cutting pin, needle or bead piercing pin
- Silver colored wire, 20 or 22 ga.
- Wire cutters, round-nose and long nose pliers
- Fine steel wool, #000 and #0000
- Two-part epoxy

Instructions

Step1. Make a template by tracing around the fired PMC diamond on an index card and cut out the shape. Set aside.

Step 2. Roll out black polymer clay on the thickest setting of pasta machine or make two stacks of 18 playing cards and roll clay out between the stacks.

Step 3. Lay the template onto clay and cut around the shape using a pin. Leave a margin of about 3/8" all around the template. Use the pin to pull the template from the cut clay being careful not to poke into the clay.

Step 4. Place PMC diamond in the center, on top of polymer diamond shape. Gently push it into the clay and bake on the Teflon sheet in a well ventilated area.

Step 5. Roll out a medium thickness piece of polymer clay (Atlas standard #4 or #5) and set aside.

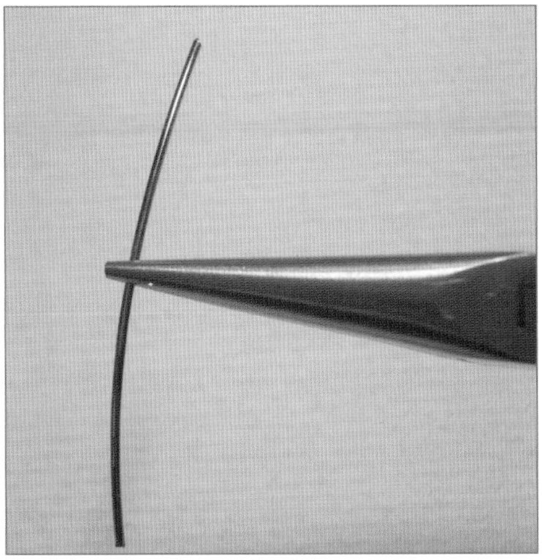

Step 6. To make wire eyes for the back of the piece: cut two pieces of wire approximately 1" long.

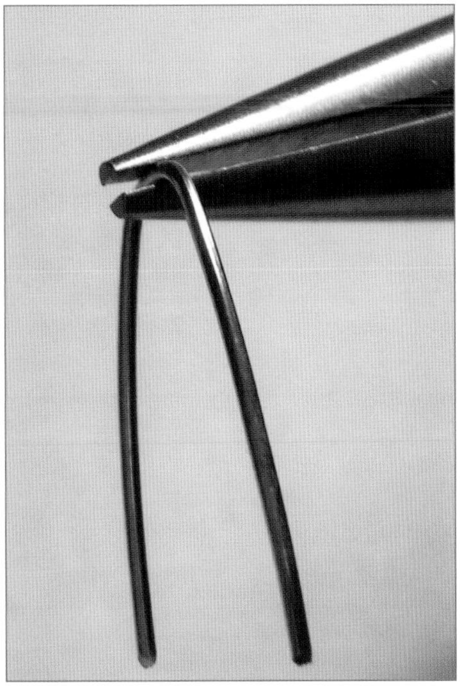

Step 7. Shape the wires into gentle C shapes...

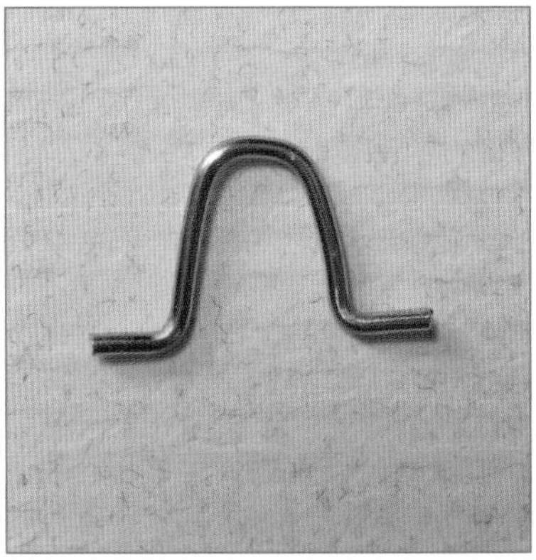

...with feet. Trim the feet to about 1/4" long making the entire wire piece approximately 1/2" long once shaped. Make two of these wire forms.

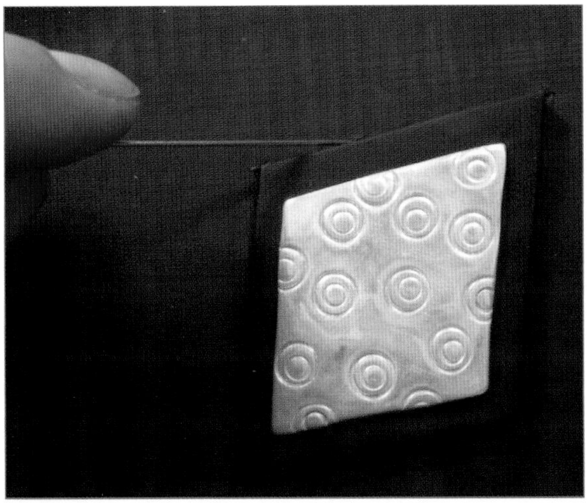

Step 8. Place cooled, baked piece onto the sheet of clay you rolled out in Step 5. Cut around the baked piece using a pin to make backing piece. Gently pry the PMC diamond piece from the polymer clay and set aside. Press the raw clay onto the baked clay piece carefully pushing out any air bubbles. Smooth raw clay over the edges to fill in seam all around the piece.

Step 9. Place one eye in position (on left or right point) on the back of the piece and push into the raw clay as far down as it will go.

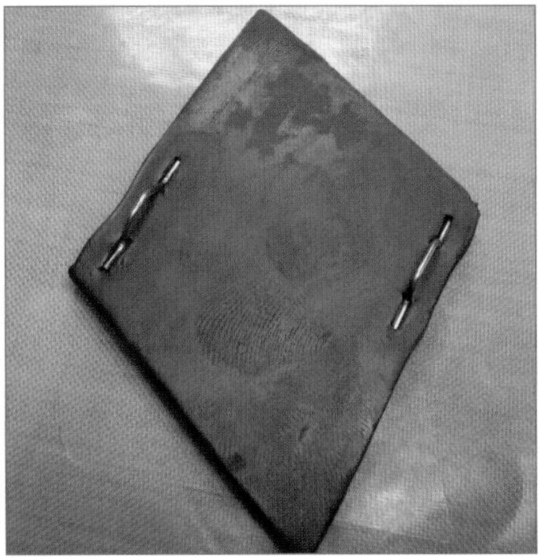

Step 10. Place second eye into position and press into place.

Step 11. Add a tiny ball of clay over the four wire feet and smooth.

Step 12. Texture the back of the piece using coarse sandpaper. Gently press the sand paper into the unbaked clay all over and around the wire eyes.

Step 13. Bake the piece at the manufacturer's suggested temperature for 30 minutes on the Teflon sheet in a well ventilated area.

Step 14. Scratch the back side of the PMC piece and apply two-part epoxy to it. Replace the PMC piece onto the baked polymer piece in position and clamp or hold in place until the epoxy sets up.

To use as a clasp for the lariat tube necklace, thread fiber wrapped elastic through the eyes on the back of the piece and knot the two ends together. The two ends of the lariat tube are fed underneath the elastic from opposite directions to hold them in place. This will leave fringe from one end of lariat pointing up and the other pointing down.

Resources

- Metal Clay: PMC3 was used in this project but Art Clay Silver can also be used. Adjust the firing temperature according to the Art Clay firing requirements so that it will sinter properly.
- Fire Mountain Gems—Art Clay Silver (www.firemountaingems.com)
- Metal Clay Supply—PMC3 (www.metalclaysupply.com)
- Bead Piercing Pins—local craft supply (Jo-Ann's, AC Moore, Michael's) (www.jewelryresourcesupply.com)
- Polymer Clay, Clay Factory (www.clayfactory.net)
- Artbeads – 3M Polishing Papers (www.artbeads.com)

Lariat

Lana May

Materials and Tools

- Seed beads size 11/0, three colors
- Swarovski crystals
- 3mm beads, two colors, 24 each
- 4mm beads, one color, 48
- 6mm beads, two colors, 8 each

Instructions

Leave the end of the thread at 10-12in. Use seed beads. Color A – silver; Color B – pink; Color C – black.

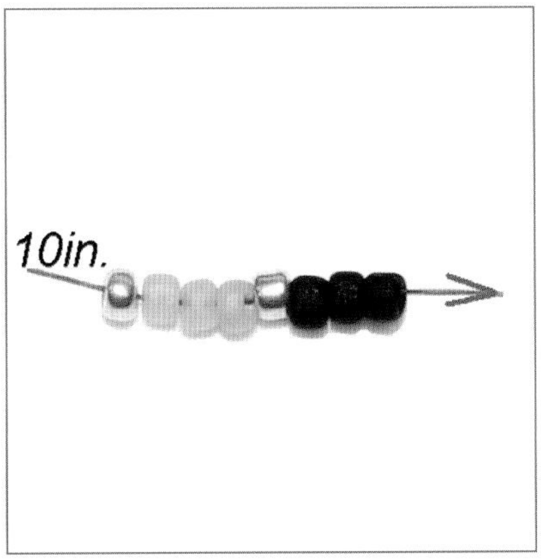

Step 1. Pick up 8 beads: A, B, B, B, A, C, C, C.

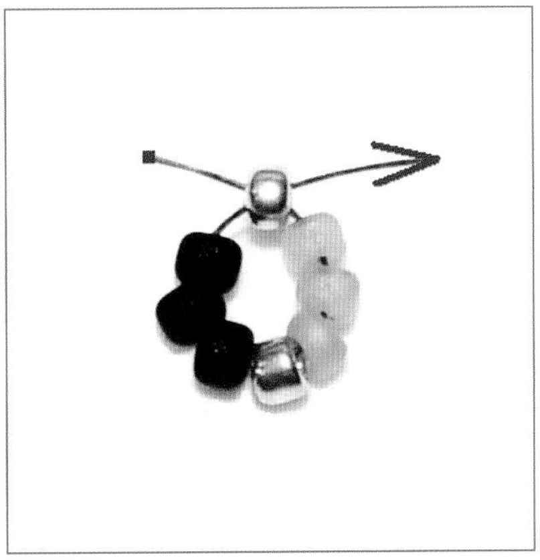

Step 2. Make a circle.

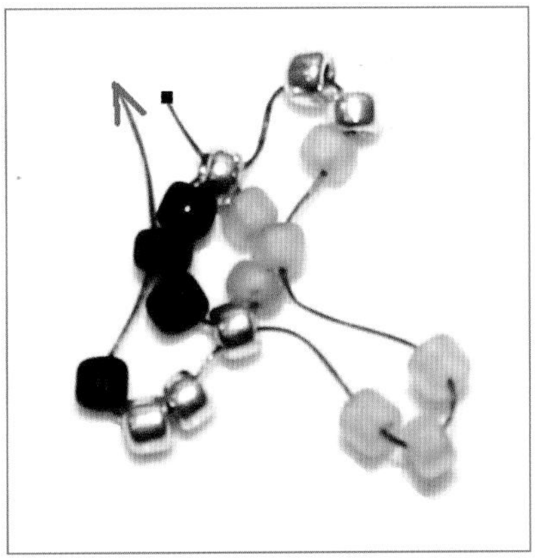

Step 3. Pick up free beads: A, A, B. Pass through middle pink.

Pick up three pink beads (B, B, B). Pass through next silver bead.

Pick up three beads: A, A, C. Pass through middle black bead

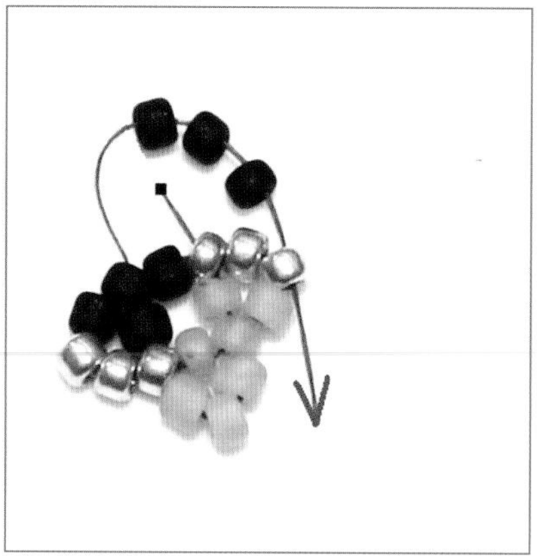

Step 4. Pick up three black beads: C, C, C. Pass through end silver bead from prevision arch.

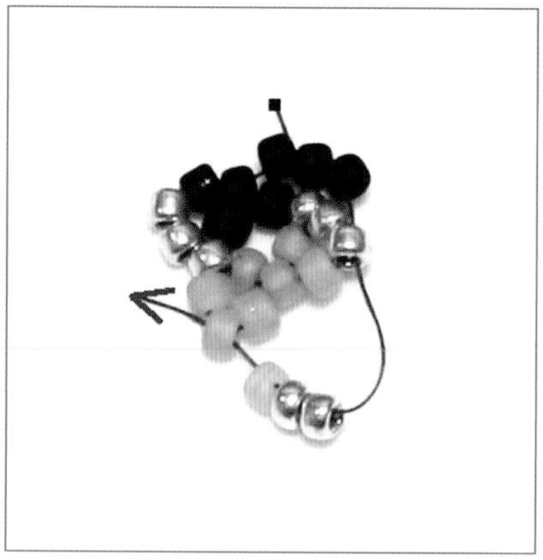

Step 5. Pick up three beads: A, A, B. Pass through middle pink bead from prevision row.

Step 6. Pick up three beads: B, B, and B. Pass through middle silver bead from prevision row.

Step 7. Pick up three beads: A, A, C. Pass through middle black bead.

Step 8. Continue netting until needed length (24-25 in)

String arch in this sequence of colors C, C, C...

...A, A, B...

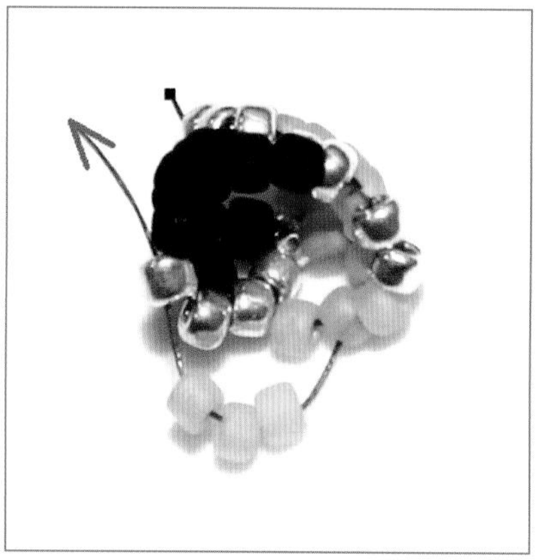

...B, B, B...

...A, A, C...

Progress

Step 9. The last time, arch only 2 beads: A, B...B, B...A, C...C, C.

Step 10. Pass through all beads from prevision row two times.

Step 11. Make fringes between beads of last row. Pick up 12 C beads, 1 A bead, 1 crystal, and 3 A beads. Pass back through the crystal, 1 A bead, and 4 B beads, then pick up 4 B beads, 1 A bead, 1 crystal, and 3 A beads. Pass back through the crystal, 4 C beads, and 4 C beads toward the tube. Pick up 6 C beads, 1 B bead, 1 crystal, and 3 B beads. Pass back through the crystal, 1 B bead, 6 C beads, and 4 C beads toward the tube, and one bead from last circle from tube.

Repeat Step 11...to make 8 fringes.

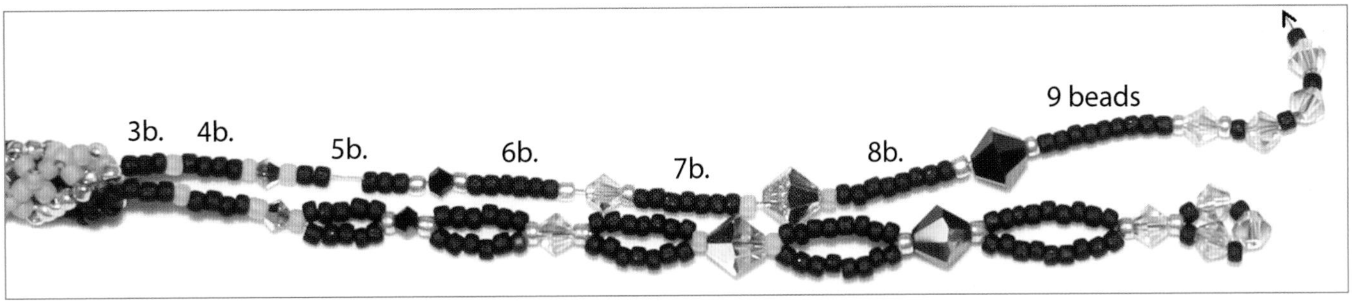

Step 12. Thread the needle with beginning 10in thread end. Look picture and string all the beads as shown on the top strand.

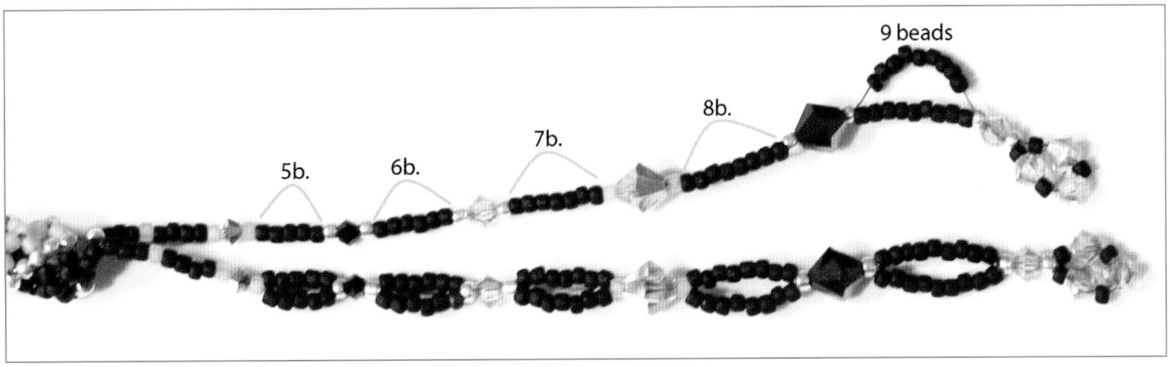

At the end, loop back through 1 A bead, 1 crystal and 1 A bead, then pick up the same number of black beads in the segment between crystals and continue doubling the chain.

Repeat to form 8 tassel fringes at the end of the tube.

The ends of the lariat tube pass through the diamond clasp.

Project 7.

Royal Necklace

Dale "Cougar" Armstrong and Olena Bugrimenko

Techniques: *wire work, chain maille*

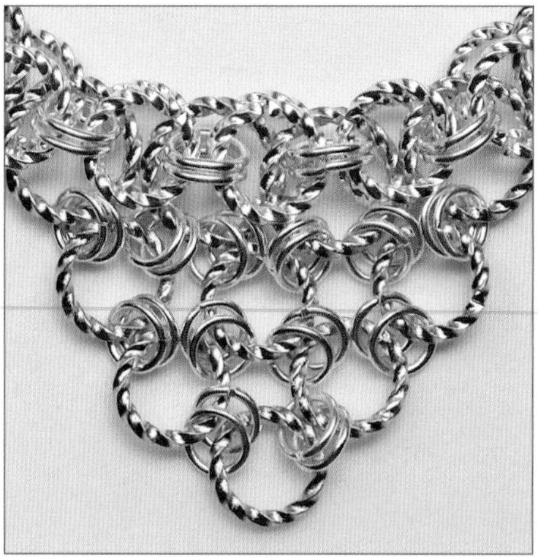

The Necklace

Olena Bugrimenko

Materials and Tools

- Jump ring twisted gold-plate 10mm 18 ga
- Jump ring twisted gold-plate 6mm 18 ga
- Jump ring twisted silver 10mm 18 ga
- Jump ring silver 6mm 18 ga
- Clasp
- Pliers
- Jump ring tool

Instructions

Step 1. First, make the central part of the necklace, beginning with a chain of 2-2-2. Slip 4 twisted silver closed rings into a small open ring. Close the open ring. Pick up a second small open ring and pass it through the 4 twisted silver closed rings. Close this open small ring.

Step 2. Open a big twisted gold ring and put it in between the twisted silver rings on each side. Do not let the gold ring go through any of the rings, just in between. Close the ring.

Step 3. Take two small open jump rings and put them around the two silver big rings on the right side. Attach two more big silver twisted rings onto the two smaller ones, then close the two open rings.

Step 4. As in Step 2, take another gold twisted big open ring and put it in between the two twisted silver rings on both sides of the jump ring that you just added. Again, do not let the gold twisted ring go through any of the other rings! Close the ring.

Step 5. Repeat steps 3-4 until you have 6 gold twisted big rings on your chain.

Khav

9544

Pickup By:
1/16/2019

Left:
Step 6. Now, attach two small silver jump rings to the second gold twisted ring on the left side. Attach 4 small silver jump rings on each of the third and fourth gold twisted rings. Then, attach two more small silver jump rings on the fifth twisted gold ring.

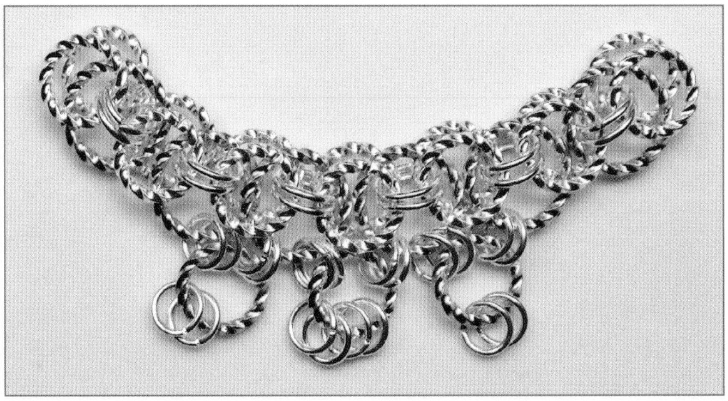

Step 7. Now open three gold large twisted rings. Each gold twisted ring will go through 4 of the small silver rings that you attached in step 6, beginning at the left and working right. Next, attach 2 small silver jump rings onto the first and third twisted gold ring that you just attached, and 4 small silver jump rings onto the middle gold twisted ring.

Step 8. Add two more gold twisted rings, make sure each gold ring is attached to 4 of the small silver rings added in Step 7! Attach two small silver jump rings to both of these gold rings. Finally, attach the last gold twisted ring, making it go through all four of the small silver rings. You are now done the central chain, congratulations!

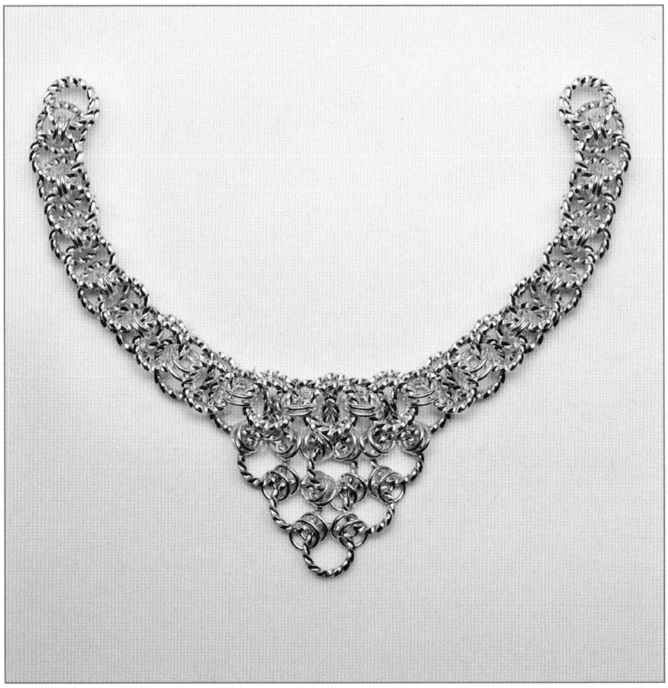

Step 9. You now repeat steps 3-5 on each side of the central part until you have reached the length you desire.

Step 10. Now attach a gold lobster clasp to one of the sides of the chain. On the other side, you make a 2-1-2 chain using two small silver jump rings and one small twisted gold ring. End in a small twisted gold ring. You can make the chain to be 3-4 inches. It regulates the length of the necklace.

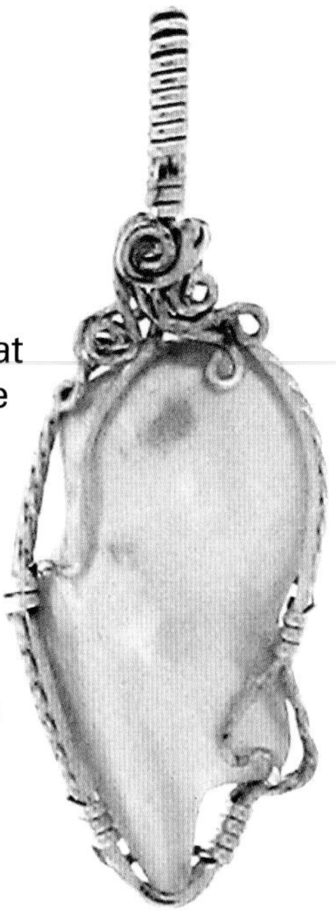

Pearl Pendant with Detachable Bail

Dale "Cougar" Armstrong

When I received this lovely necklace from Olena, I knew that whatever pendant design I choose to make for it would have to be very special, yet not take away from the chain maille design. Looking through my many boxes of designer cabochons, not one caught my eye until I remembered one of my favorite materials, pearls! Yes, a pearl emanates classic elegance whether worn with blue jeans or velvet, but what if the owner wanted to be a bit more casual? The answer was to make this design with a specialty bail that allows the pendant to be removed. Therefore the featured technique in this wired pendant design is the "detachable bail."

Skill Level: Advanced Intermediate

Materials and Tools

- 22 gauge square half-hard wire, (main frame)
- 22g square dead soft, (top frame wire only)
- 20 gauge half-round, half-hard wire, (wrap wire)
- 1- freeform pearl
- Flat-nose pliers
- Round-nose pliers
- Chain-nose pliers
- Angle cutters
- Double barrel bail pliers
- Pin vise
- Quilter's tape
- Ruler
- Ultra fine point marker

Instructions

Frame Formula:
Circumference of pearl + 3 inches = length of 22g wire
Number of 22g wires = enough to cover the side of the pearl + 2

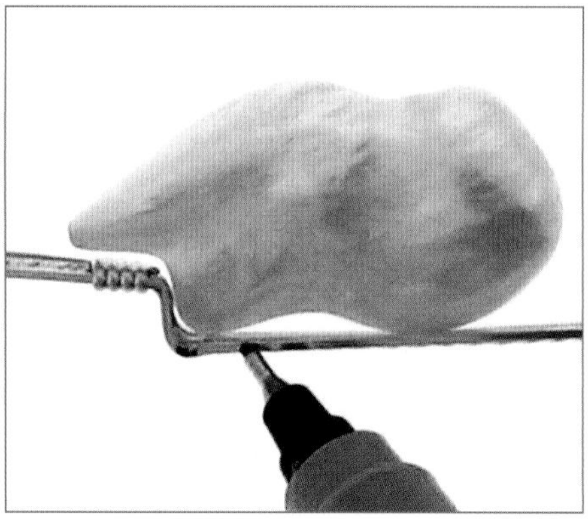

Step 1. Straighten, clean, measure and then cut all necessary 22g wires according to the formula. (If desired, twist one or two of these wires as shown). Place all of the 22g wires side-by-side with the one soft wire on one edge, which will be used on the top of the pendant. Tape near each end, forming a "bundle." Find the center of the bundle and mark across it. Then measure and mark 1/8-inch on each side of the center mark. Wrap a 6-inch piece of 20g 1/2- round, 1/2-hard wire across the entire center, from one side mark to the other, (about 4 wraps-to-show).

Step 2. Place the pearl alongside the wire bundle and, while shaping the frame, decide where to place the additional wraps.

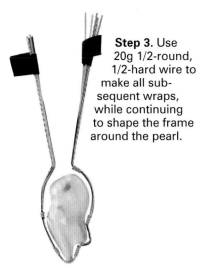

Step 3. Use 20g 1/2-round, 1/2-hard wire to make all subsequent wraps, while continuing to shape the frame around the pearl.

Step 4. Remove all tape and working "off the stone," bring the frame together and tape about 1-inch above the junction. Straighten and cut one 3-inch piece of 22g square 1/2-hard wire to use for the main bail wrap. Begin at the top of the frame and wrap up and away from the frame junction, 3 times to show and trim. Remove the tape.

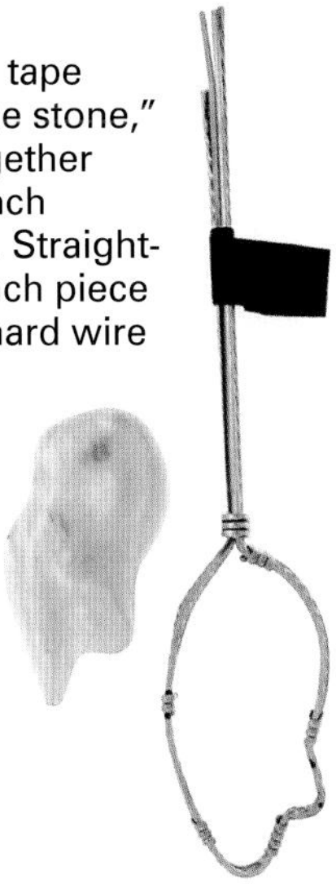

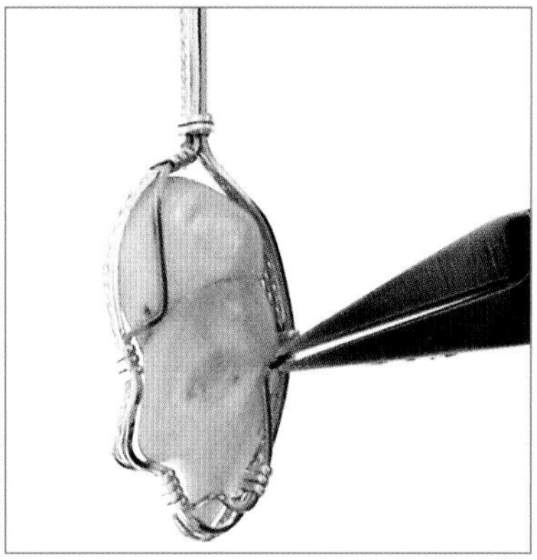

Step 5. Place the pearl into the frame. On the back, beginning at the bottom center, use flat-nose pliers to grasp the topmost wire immediately next to a wrap and roll the pliers toward the pearl at a 45° to 90° angle. Repeat at all points necessary to form a back platform to secure the pearl.

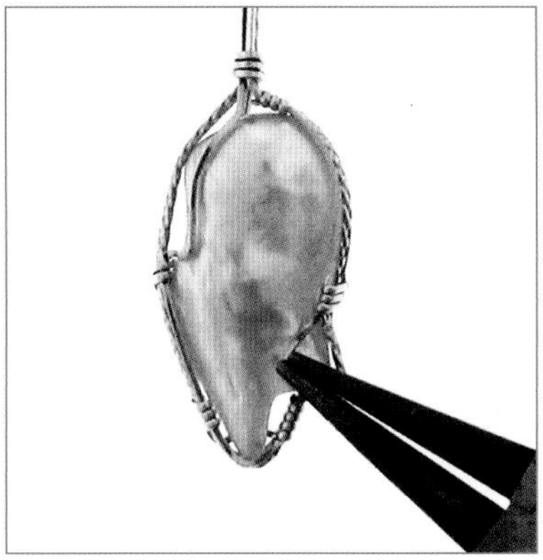

Step 6. On the front of the pendant, use chain-nose or round-nose (or a combination of both) to repeat Step 5, making angles/curves to flow with the pearl and lock it into the pendant frame.

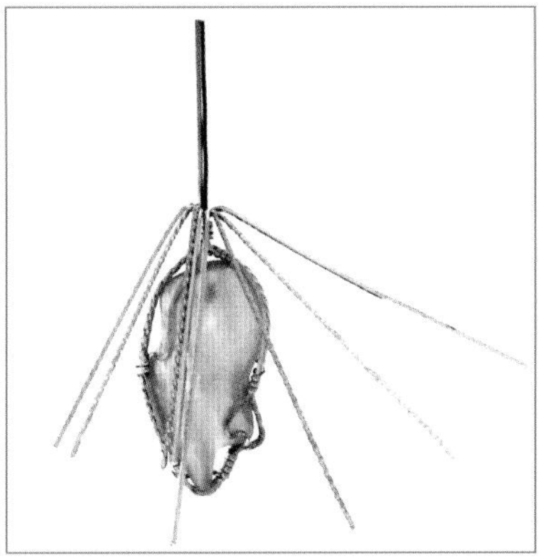

Step 7. At the top of the pendant, bring all but the last two wires, (one on each side), to the front. Trim these two wires to 1-inch long; these are now the "bail" wires.

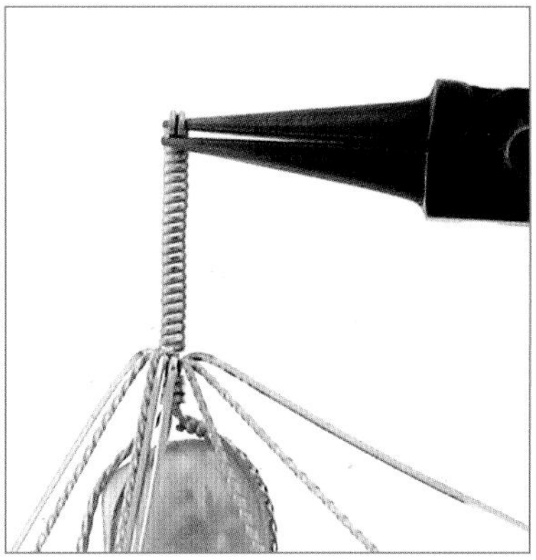

Step 8. Use flat-nose pliers and a 5-inch length of 20g 1/2-round, 1/2-hard wire, to wrap the two bail wires together, (beginning and ending on the front), up to 3/4-inch from the main bail wrap, and trim. Place the tips of chain-nose pliers at the end of the unwrapped bail wires and roll back toward the pendant, forming a tiny, closed loop.

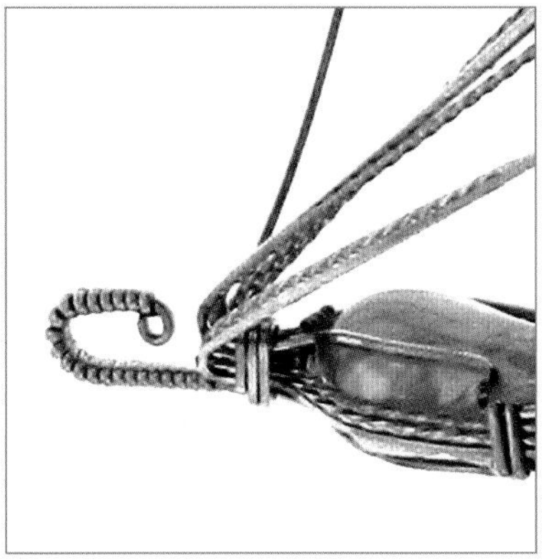

Step 9. Using a small round jawed tool, place it 1/4-inch away from the looped end and roll the pliers toward the front of the pendant. This forms the "detachable" bail.

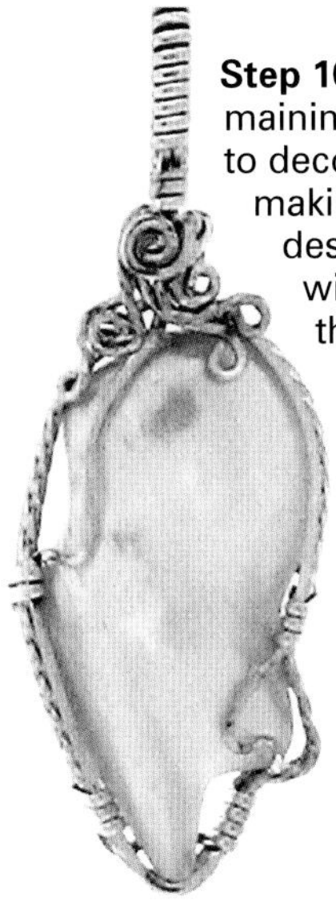

Step 10. Return to the remaining wires and use them to decorate as desired, making sure the chosen design does not interfere with being able to use the bail.

Step 11. Slip the bail through the bottom/center jump ring on the chain maille necklace.

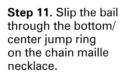

Project 8.

"The Ancient's Civilization" Bracelet

Kathy St. Martin and Olena Bugrimenko

Techniques: *PMC, wire work, and chain maille*

Three-Piece Dome Pendent

Kathy St. Martin

Materials and Tools

- Basic setup using notebook sleeve with very heavy card stock
- Rolling pin
- Light bulb
- Two stack of playing cards, 2-3 cards thick
- Various textured surfaces
- PMC+ 18gram lump clay
- 1′ 20Gage 1/2 hard SS wire
- Cool Slip coating
- Marker & ruler

Instructions

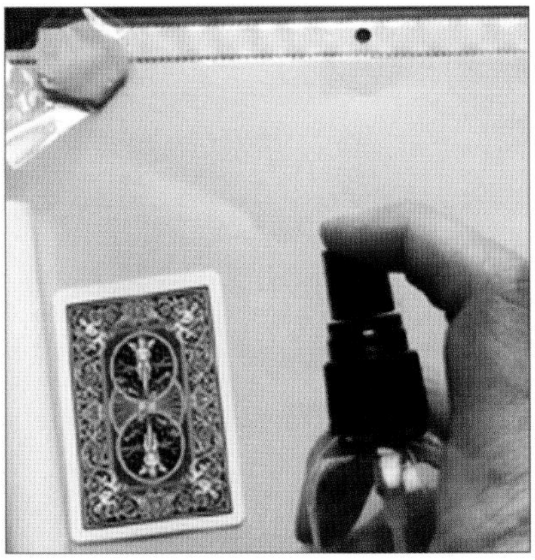

Step 1. Lightly coat surface between cards, rolling pin, hands, and the textured surfaces with Cool Slip. Take 1/3 of lump clay. Roll in hands to blend, removing all cracks. Place between cards and prep for rolling.

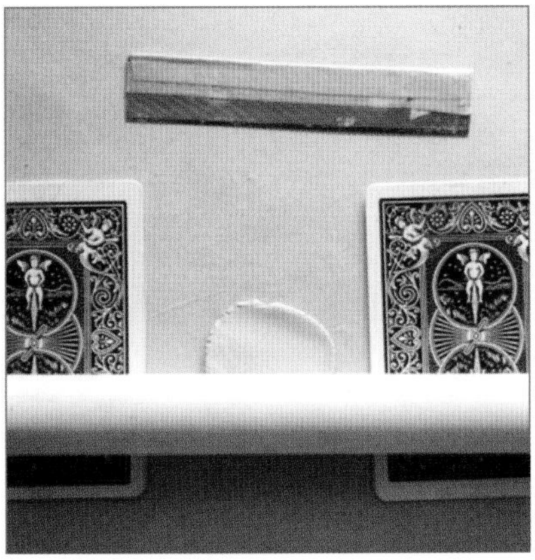

Step 2. Roll out clay evenly to approximately 2mm above height of the cards. Set the rolled out clay on top of the textured surface.

Step 3. Press firmly from center of clay outward leaving an ample, even thickness so you can peel up later. Again roll from center toward opposite direction.

Step 4. Peel and remove the textured clay and place it on a lighted bulb to give it a rounded shape.

Step 5. Place the clay and the light bulb in a dehydrator covering it very carefully.

Step 6. Using your second coated textured surface and a good chunk of clay, roll piece as above and repeat the process, including drying, though you may omit the light bulb on these pieces.

Repeat this step so you have two similar pieces of the same size.

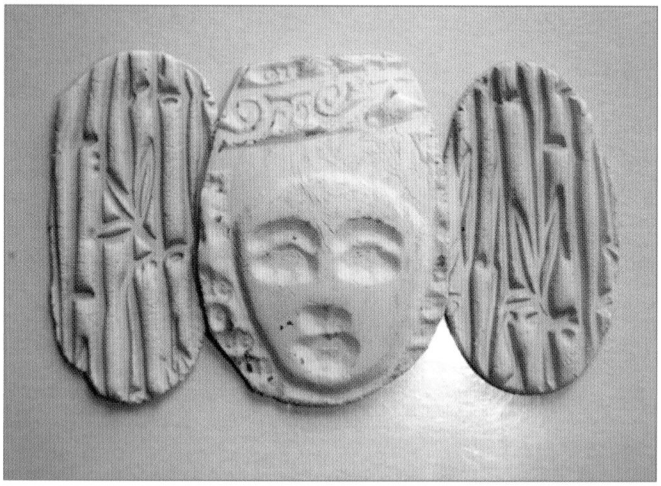

Step 7. Once all three pieces are dry, line them up overlapping the side pieces with the center piece to get an initial idea of how they will fit together.

Sanding

Step 8. Use an emery board, sand the parameters of all three pieces. You can shape the pieces at the same time. Sand on an angle for a nice beveled effect.

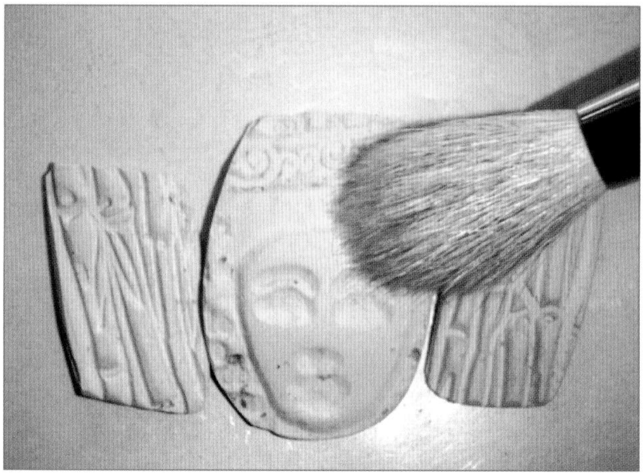

Step 9. Brush off all fine clay powder.

Making Holes

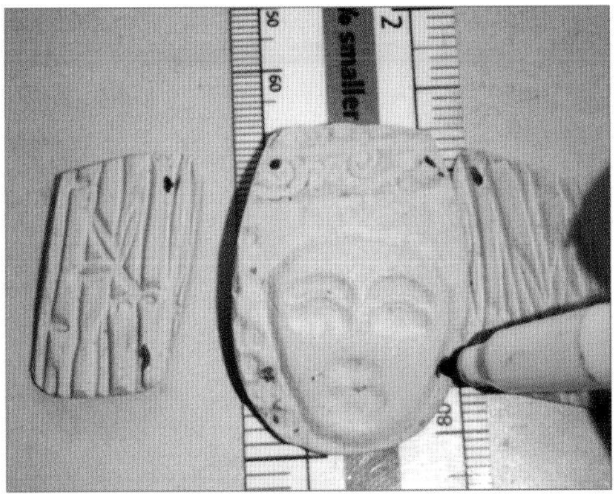

Step 10. Set center piece on top of a ruler. Mark all four corners for drilling, using the ruler to make sure the two sides match. Hand drill the four holes in the dry clay.

Step 11. Set center piece on top of side pieces. Mark the holes on the side pieces and drill at the marks. Add two outer holes on each side piece.

Torch Firing

Step 12. The torch set up includes: one 6" clay plant tray, 3-4oz of vermiculite, a honey comb soldering block, fiber board, tongs, soldering pick, and a butane torch. An igniter is optional.

Step 13. Place the pieces on top of the vermiculite.

Step 14. Fire pieces evenly until pale orange in color. Three pieces take more time to get to this point than one does, due to thickness and size. Once pale orange, time the flame for 4 minutes. Note: Hold torch 1-1/2" from the pieces and use a circular motion.

Tumble

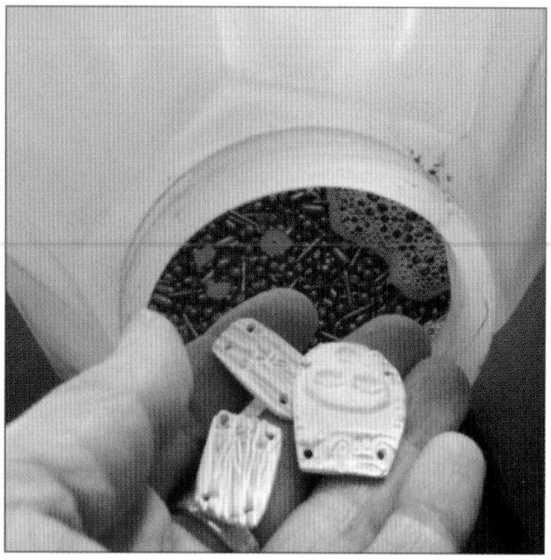

Step 15. Tumble for 1 hour with mixed steel shot and standard liquid soap and water. You can opt for hand polishing using Radial Discs from Rio Grande.

Beaded Joints

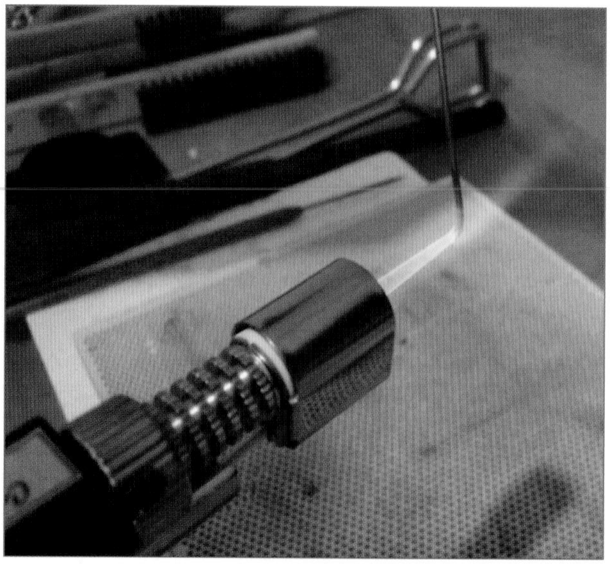

Step 16. Cut 20 or 18 gage SS wire to 3″ lengths. Make four pieces. Using torch and holding the end of a piece of wire, watch the torch bead up the opposite end. Repeat soldering with remainder 3 wires.

Step 17. Insert a wire in each stacked drilled hole from the front. Turn piece up-side-down and using the torch bead each wire as close to the piece as possible.

Step 18. Hand polish each beaded wire.

Step 19. The pendent will attach to the bracelet.

Bracelet

Olena Bugrimenko

Materials and Tools

- Jump rings, 5mm, 18ga
- Headpins
- Earpins
- Hematite beads 6mm
- Hematite slider 18 x 10mm
- Clasp
- Pliers
- Jump ring tool

Instructions

Step 1. Prepare the Hematite slider so you can attach it to the bracelet. Put eyepins in each of the 2 holes in the slider. Make a basic loop on the end of each eyepin. Repeat this on the second slider. In the same way, prepare the Hematite beads by putting each one on an eyepin and making a basic loop on the end. You need to make seven more of these. At the top center of the photo is the Hematite clasp.

Step 2. Make a 2-2-2 chain of jump rings. Pick up an open ring and slip 4 closed rings into it. Close the open ring. Pass a second open ring through the 4 closed rings, and close it.

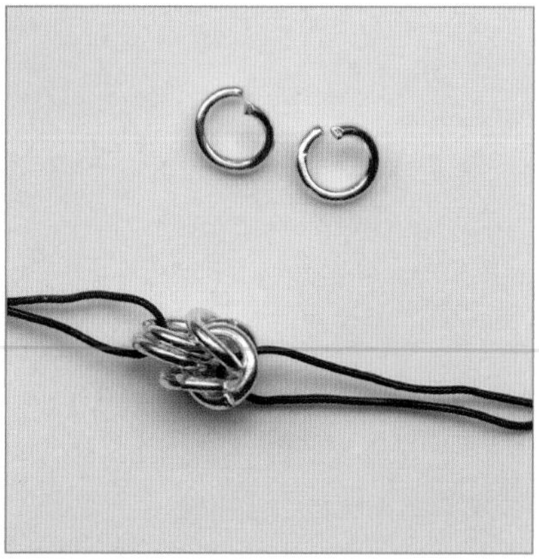

Step 3. Hold the 2 closed rings that are on the left side. Move the 2 closed rings on the right in opposite directions around the middle rings, so they rest against the rings on the left. For the next step, open 2 rings.

Step 4. Insert the two open rings, between the two original middle rings and through the two rings that are resting against the left rings. Open 2 more rings.

Step 5. Add the two open rings to the two you just added. Open 2 more rings.

Step 6. Add the two additional rings to those you just added.

Step 7. To make the right side look like the left, turn the end rings back toward the middle and grab them between the two rings that were on their left.

Step 8. Add two rings to this spot to finish the first segment

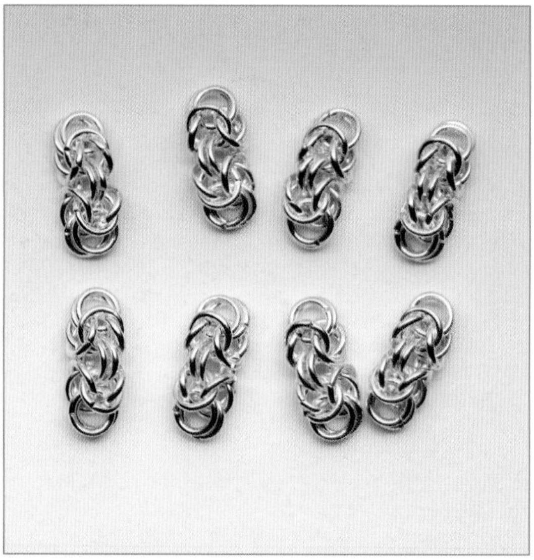

Step 9. You need to make seven more.

Step 10. Attach all chains to the beads, the sliders, and the pendant. Add the clasp. You have now created the bracelet!

Project 9.

"Blue Spark" Necklace

Lana May & Irina Serbina

Techniques: *beaded beads, macramé*

Project 9

Set of Beaded Beads

Lana May

Materials and Tools

- Seed beads size 14/0 5gr;
- Seed beads size 11/0 15gr;
- Seed beads size 8/0 5gr;
- Drops 3mm 5gr;
- Swarovski crystal bicone:
- 2mm (63+ 49 = 112beads)
- 4 mm (28+20 = 48beads);
- 5mm (14+10 = 24beads);
- 6mm (14+5 =19 beads);
- 8mm (7beads)
- Needle, size #10;
- Fire Line 8lb.

Instructions

Big Beaded Bead

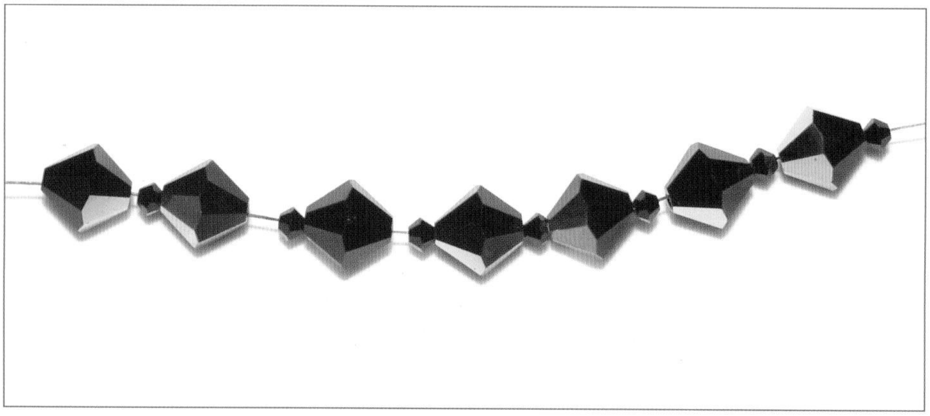

Step 1. On a thread about 15in. long string a series of 14 beads, seven of each size. The pattern is 1 bead 8mm, 1 bead 2mm, 1 bead 8mm, 1 bead 2mm, 1 bead 8mm, and so forth.

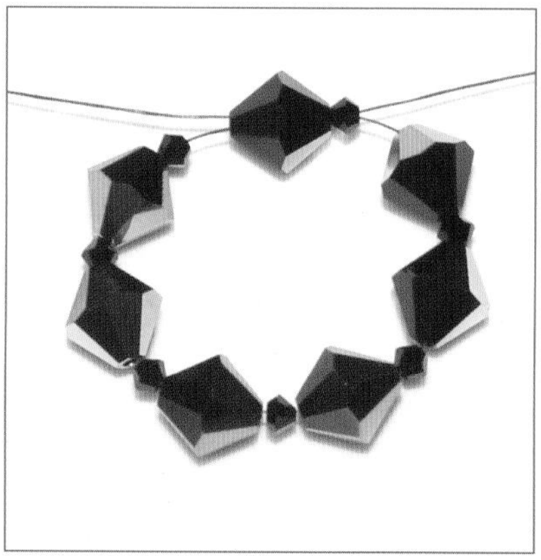

Step 2. Make a circle, passing the thread through first two beads: 8mm and 2mm.

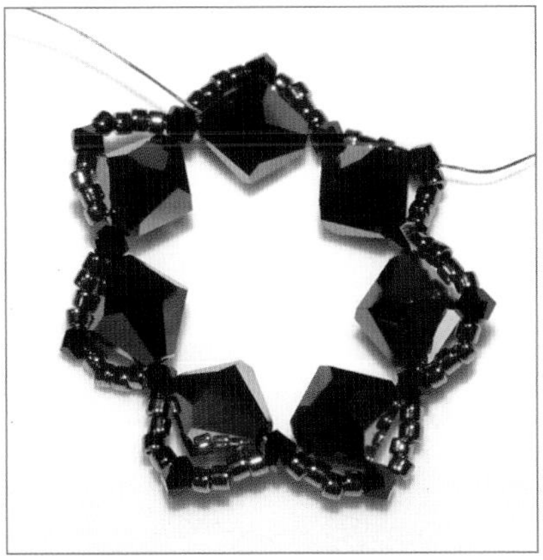

Step 3. Pick up 4 seed beads, 1 bead 2mm, and 4 seed beads. Pass through bead 2mm from first row that is between 2 beads 8mm. Repeat this 7 times. Last time pass though first 4 seed beads and bead 2mm from this row.

Step 4. Pick up 1 bead 6mm between beads 2mm from step 3. Pick up a total of 7 beads 6mm, finishing by going through the bead 2mm.

Step 5. Pick up 3 seed beads, bead 2mm, and 3 seed beads. Pass through bead 2mm between beads 6mm. Repeat this 7 times. Last time pass through first 3 seed beads and bead 2mm from this row.

Step 6. Pick up bead 5mm between beads 2mm from step 5, adding 7 beads and finishing by passing through a bead 2mm.

Step 7. Pick up bead 3mm, bead 2mm, and 3mm. Pass through bead 2mm between beads 5mm. Repeat this 7 times. Last time pass through first bead 3mm and bead 2mm

Step 8. Pick up seed bead, bead 2mm, and seed bead between beads 2mm from Step 7.

Step 9. Make the loops. Pick up 5 seed beads size 11/0. Pass through 5 beads from Step 8: seed bead, bead 2mm, seed bead, bead 2mm, and seed bead. Repeat this around the top circle. Pass through 2-3 beads. Make knots between beads. Cut thread.

Step 10. Turn the work over. Return to the first row of beads 8mm. Thread needle. Repeat Steps 3 through 8.

Step 11. Instead of the small loops in Step 9, make big loops. Pick up six seed beads size 14/0, six seed beads size 11/0, three seed beads size 8/0, drop bead, two seed beads size 8/0, two seed beads size11/0, and two seed beads size 14/0. Pass through five beads from last row: seed bead, bead 2mm, seed bead, bead 2mm, and seed bead. Make these loops around bottom circle.

Small Beaded Bead

Use the same technique for small beaded bead.

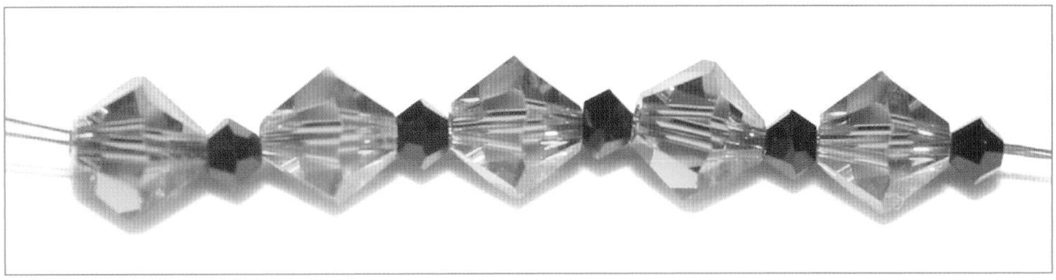

Step 1. Start with a 15in thread. String 10 beads: Bead 6mm, bead 2mm, bead 6mm, bead 2mm, and so on, repeating each size 5 times.

Left:
Step 3. Pick up 3 seed beads, bead 2mm, and 3 seed beads. Pass through bead 2mm from first row. Repeat this 5 times. Last time pass though first 3 seed beads and bead 2mm from this row.

Step 2. Make a circle. Pass through first two beads: 6mm and 2mm.

Step 4. Pick up bead 5mm between beads 2mm from Step 3.

Step 5. Pick up bead 3mm, bead 2mm, and bead 3mm. Pass through bead 2mm between beads 5mm. Repeat this 5 times. Last time pass through first bead 3mm and bead 2mm.

Step 6. Pick up seed bead, bead 2mm, and seed bead between beads 2mm from step 5.

Step 7. Make the loops. Pick up 5 seed beads size 11/0. Pass through 5 beads: seed bead, bead 2mm, seed bead, bead 2mm, and seed bead. Repeat this on the top circle. Pass through 2-3 beads. Make knots between beads. Cut thread.

Step 8. Turn over the work. Starting with the first row of beads 6mm repeat steps 3 through 7. Make 2 small beaded beads.

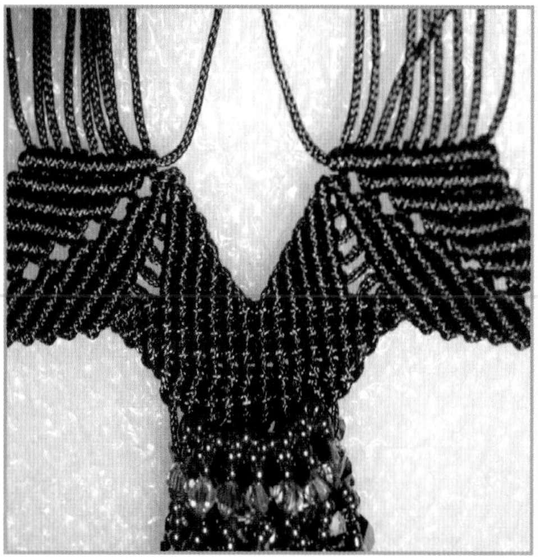

Macramé Necklace

Irina Serbina

Materials and Tools

- Scissors.
- Working surface. (Firm surface, to which your work can be pinned down: poly-foam, cork, or polyurethane.
- Long straight pins (T-pins work great)
- 12" piece of a heavy SoftFlex or Beadalon, to help you get your knotting cord through the hole of some beads.
- Ten pieces of 10ft of Chinese Knotting cord, and three to five 3 ft pieces.
- Clasp of your choice.

Instructions

Step 1. Start your necklace by creating a "tassel" with 5 long (10 ft) and 3-5 short (3 ft) strands of cord. Fold each long cord in half, then string a bead on each long cord and move it to the middle. Pin down the bead and knot 3" to 5" of half-knots on each cord.

Tip: to make it easier to string your beads, you can either soak the end of a cord with superglue, or "melt" it with lighter and pull ends with wet fingers while still hot, creating a "needle end" on each cord.

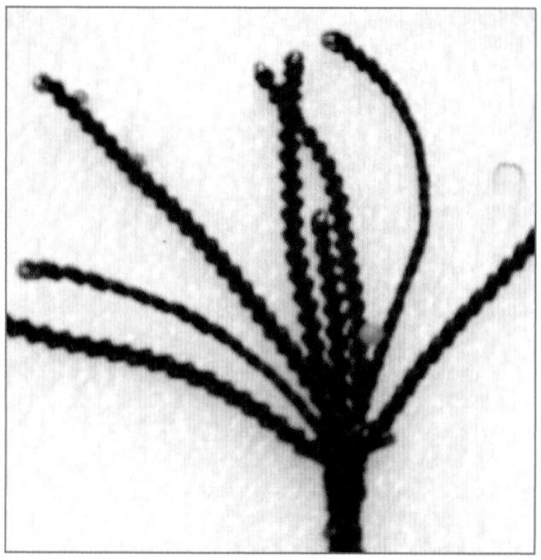

Step 2. Gather all created chains together in a tassel, and make a couple of square knots using two longest cords as "working cords" and the rest as "filler cords." Add a drop of glue inside the square knot, let it dry. Trim the remaining ends of the short cords. You will have 10 long working cords left to work with.

1. Left half Knot

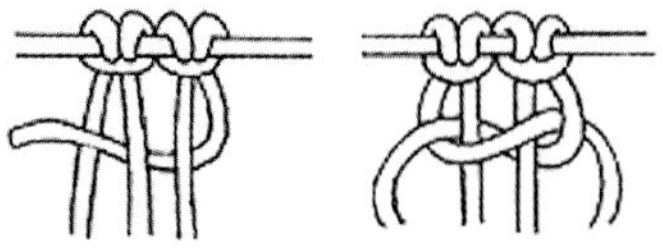

2. Right Half Knot

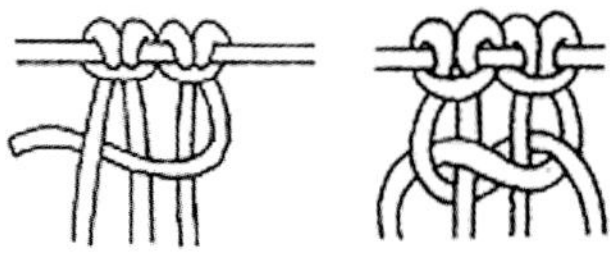

3. Complete Square Knot

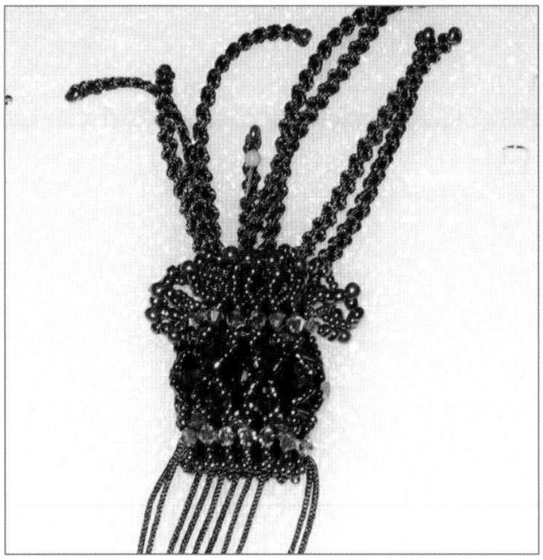

Step 3. Pull all long cords through the big bead, driving two cords on each side through the hole close to the top edge of the bead, to make sure bead does not slide down. You should get 10 "working cords"

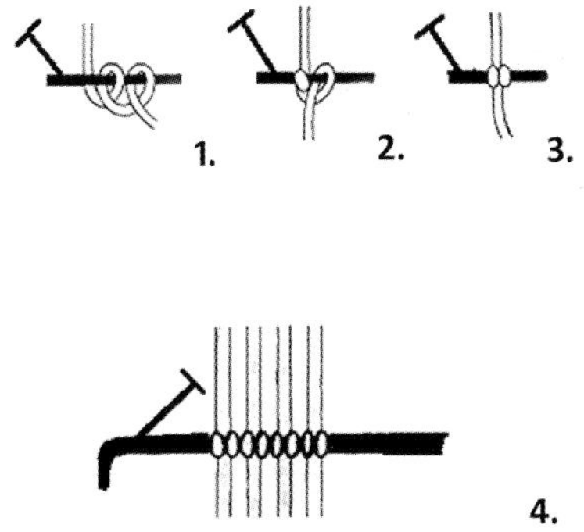

Step 4. Place short cord horizontally across all your working cords; it will become your anchor cord. Pin down the middle of the cord to the left of your work. Clove hitch horizontally across the other cords.

Step 5. Bring both ends of your anchor cord down and align them with your knotting cords. You have now 12 knotting cords for the next clove hitch row. Place a new short cord across all your cords, pin it down on the left, work to the right making a second row of clove hitch knots. Make sure it is tied close to the top row, and the anchor cord is pulled taut all the time. Repeat this step with the rest of your short cords, until you have added all your cords. The result is seen here.

Step 6. Turn your work over, split the twenty cords in two equal parts.

- With cord number 9 as an anchor, use cord 10 to make a vertical clove hitch knot.
- With cord 8 as an anchor, use cords 9 and 10 to make two vertical clove hitch knots.
- With cord 7 as an anchor, use cords 8, 9 and 10 for a line of vertical clove hitch knots.
- With cord 6 as an anchor, use cords 7 through 10 for a line of vertical clove hitch knots
- With cord 5 as an anchor, use cords 6 through 10 for a line of vertical clove hitch knots

Repeat the same process on the other side:

- Begin with cord 12 as an anchor and use cord 11 to make a vertical clove hitch knot.
- With cord 13 as an anchor, use cords 10-11 for a line of vertical clove hitch knots
- Repeat on cords 14, 15, and 16.

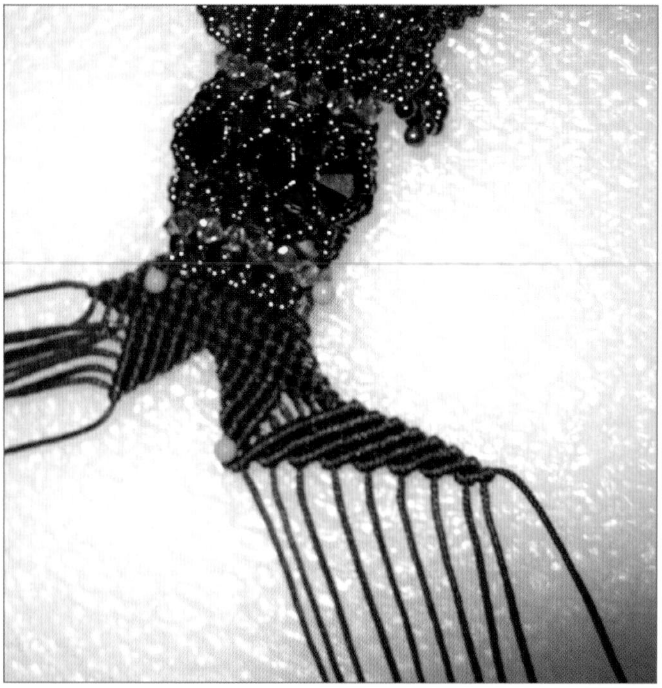

Step 7. Pin your work at an angle, as shown on the picture. Working on the right side:

- Use the left cord as an anchor and make a line of 9 horizontal clove hitch knots.
- Use the second cord as an anchor and make a line of 8 horizontal clove hitch knots.
- Use the third cord and make a line of 7 horizontal clove hitch knots.
- Continue the process with 6 knots on fourth cord
- 5 knots on fifth cord
- 4 knots on sixth cord
- 3 knots on seventh cord
- 2 knots on eighth cord

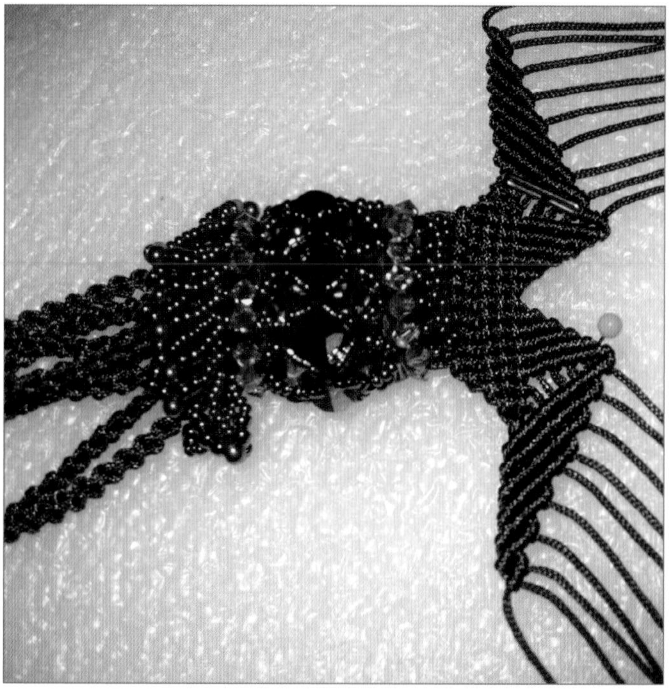

Step 8. Turn your work to pin it down as shown on the picture and repeat previous step on the left side, working from right to left.

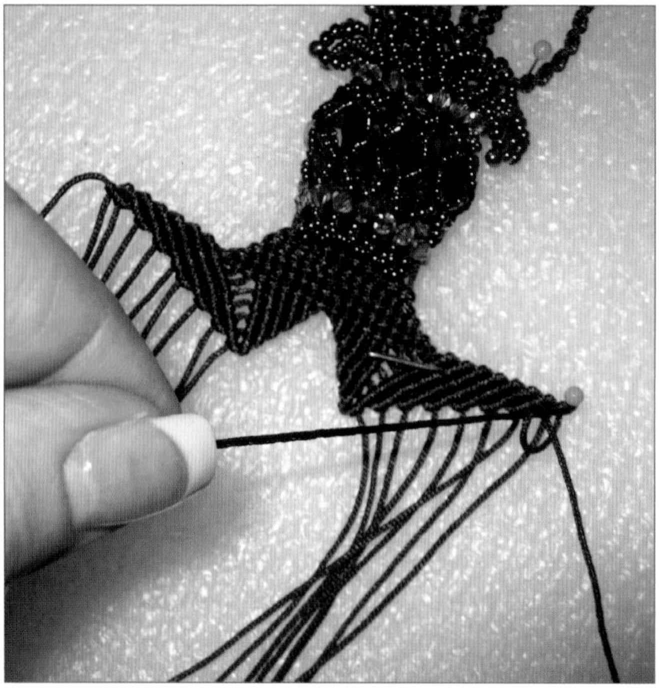

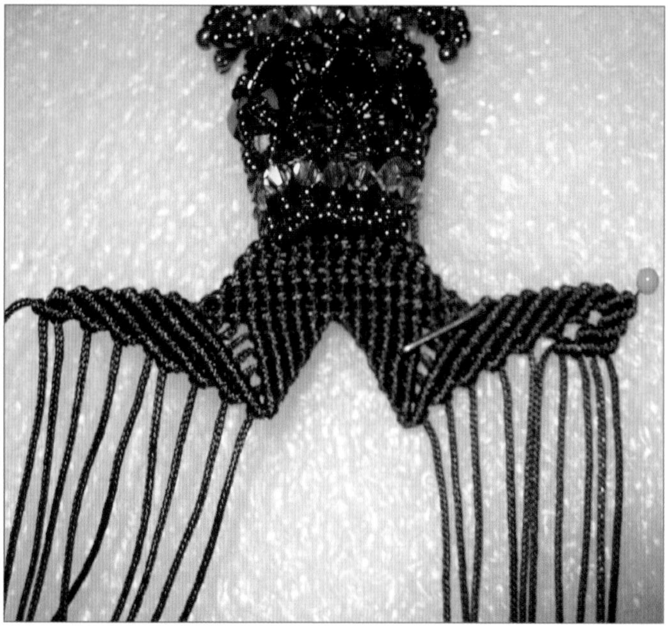

Left and above:
Step 9. Repin the work again, as shown:

- Line 1: using your foremost right cord as an anchor, make a line of 2 horizontal clove hitch knots, working from right to left.
- Line 2: using the right cord make a line of 3 horizontal clove hitch knots, adding the 3rd working cord from the previous row.
- Line 3: line of 4 knots
- Line 4: line of 5 knots

Continue until the "leaf design" looks symmetrical.

Tip: *when you are doing the last knot in each row, pull anchor cord all the way up to the previous row, to make the new line sit snug against the upper half of the leaf. There should be no loose cord hanging in the middle of the leaf – only "diamond" shaped holes between the lines.*

Step 10. Finish the leaf design on the other side by tying the horizontal clove hitch knots from left to right, starting with 2 knots and increasing till you get last line of 9 knots.

Step 11. Turn your work over. Make a line of 3 clove hitch knots using 4th cord from the middle as an anchor, holding it at 45 degrees to the previous line

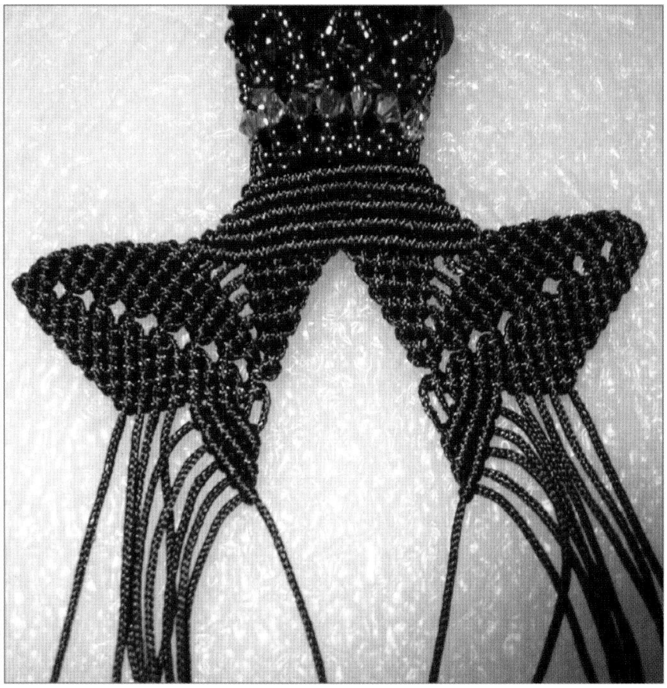

Step 12. Make two more lines of clove hitch knots at 45 degrees on cords number 5 and 6 on both sides.

Step 13. Turn your work over. Make two lines of clove hitch knots (snug to the previous line) on cords 7 and 8.

Step 15. Turn your work over again.
• Line 1. Make a line of 8 knots using foremost left cord as an anchor.
• Line 2. Make a line of 6 knots using **two** foremost left cords as an anchor.
• Line 3. Make a line of 4 knots using **two** foremost left cords as an anchor.
• Line 4. Make a line of 2 knots using **two** foremost left cords as an anchor.
Mirror the same steps on the other side of the necklace.

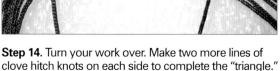

Step 14. Turn your work over. Make two more lines of clove hitch knots on each side to complete the "triangle."

Right:
Step 16. Turn your work over to have your necklace facing down. Make an 8" chain of alternating left and right half hitch knots on each pair of cords. *[see Step 1 for a diagram of alternating left and right half hitch knots]*

Far right:
Step 17. Slide smaller beads over the chains on each side of the necklace. They should freely slide over the chains and stop at the beginning of design. If they were made too loose and slide further, attach them at this point with either glue or a needle and matching thread.

Step 18. Attach a clasp. Pick the 2 longest cords remaining on each side, slide them in the opposite directions into the clasp loop, fold ends down and make a sinnet of 3-4 square knots using all the rest of the cords as filler cords. Add glue inside the knots, then tie and trim the edges.

Tip: You can hide ends of the working cords INSIDE the sinnet. Add two cords of a contrasting color, folded in half, to the filler cords. After completing 3-4 square knots, pull one of the ends of the working cords half way through the loop of the contrasting cord and pull the loop up through the sinnet. Repeat the same step with the other working cord. Add a drop of glue inside the last square knot; cut excess cord.

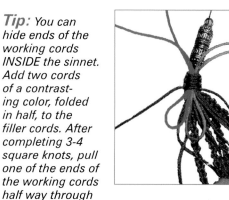

Gallery

Combining jewelry-making techniques gives a great opportunity for a piece to be unique, beautiful, and sophisticated. When you're creating a piece of jewelry this way, you get to meet new people who may become lifelong friends, that share the same interests as you. And good friends just bring you one step closer to living a good, happy life. Please look at my friends' galleries.

"Bahamas Mermaid" Necklace
by Tatiana Van Iten
Techniques: *bead netting, bead embroidery, wire work*

"Bling" Bracelet by Jean Campbell
Techniques: *right-angle weave, peyote stitch, wirework*

Necklace with glass bead by Olena Bugrimenko and Laurie Nessel
Techniques: *crocheting, glass flame work*

"Spring" Necklace
by Tatiana Van Iten
Techniques: *peyote stitch, crocheting*

"Mermaid's Adornment"
by Meredith Arnold and Kathy St. Martin
Techniques: *PMC, liquid polymer clay medium*

"Orchid" Necklace by Olena Bugrimenko
Techniques: *crocheting, beading, wiring.*

"Inca's Gold" Necklace by Albina Manning
Techniques: *wire work, chain maille.*

Set made by Tatiana Van Iten
Techniques: *wire crochet, bead netting*

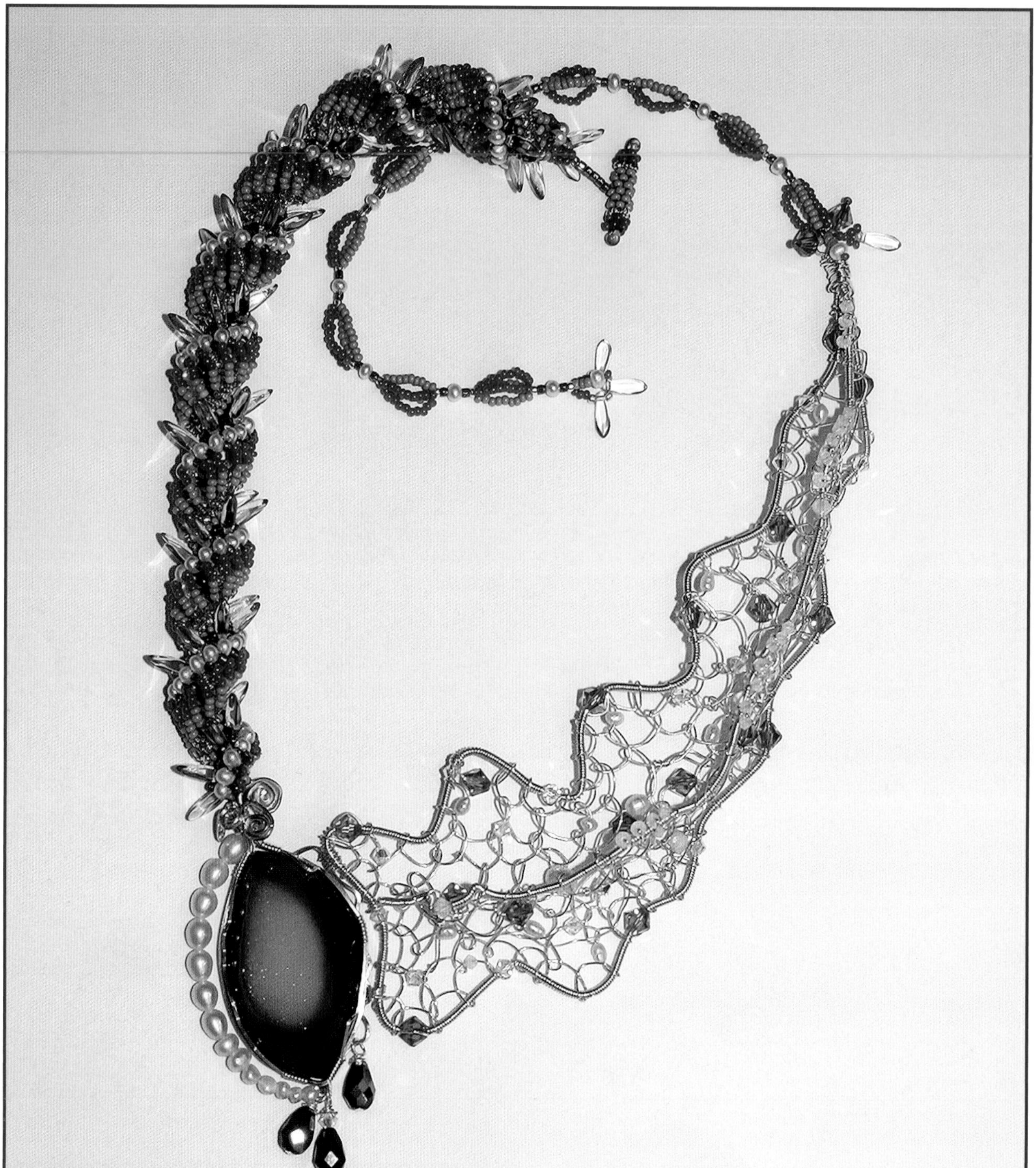

Necklace Ocean made by Olena Bugrimenko and Lana May
Techniques: *wire work and beaded tube.*

Photo by Gleb Serbin, www.gserbin.smugmug.com

"Melting Icicles" Necklace by Kathy St Martin and Lana May
Techniques: *PMC, beading techniques*

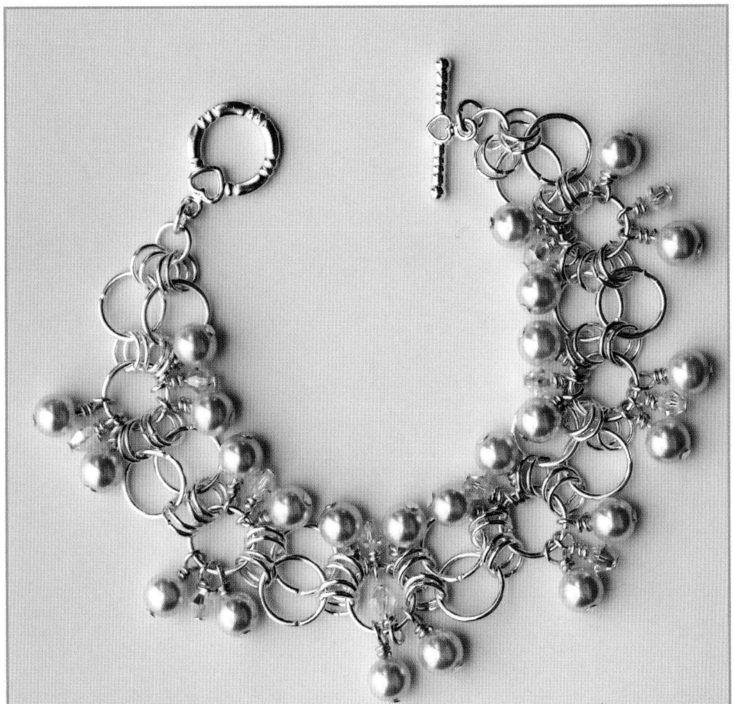

"Joyous life" Bracelet by Olena Bugrimenko
Techniques: *chain maille, wiring (wire wrapped)*

"Gita Maria" Necklace by Tatiana Van Iten
Techniques: *bead netting, bead embroidery, wire work*

"Smoke on Water" Necklace by Tatiana Van Iten
Techniques: *wire crochet, bead netting, Russian leaves, and fringes*

About the Instructors

Dale "Cougar" Armstrong is a diehard rockhound, lapidary, and a full-time wire jewelry artist, instructor and author, with a background in cloisonné and repoussé prior to making wire jewelry. With more than 35 years of combined experience, Dale uses absolutely no solder or glue in her classic wire jewelry designs, and teaches how at national jewelry making events across the country. Her award winning work is sold in galleries and gift shops and has appeared in many printed publications. Author of the best selling book, *Wirework: An Illustrated Guide to the Art of Wire Wrapping*, she has also made a series of instructional DVDs for Jewelry Television, and has appeared on the PBS broadcast show "Beads, Baubles & Jewels." Dale "Cougar" is the face of www.Wire-Sculpture.com having joined their team in June 2009, and has just completed an extended series of instructional DVDs with their new company. Contact via website: www.cougarscreations.com

Meredith Arnold is a comedian-artist specializing in jewelry and mixed media. Her work has been published in many books and magazines and is exhibited nationally.

As a professional teaching artist, Meredith teaches around the U.S. for Interweave Press and appears on the PBS show "Beads, Baubles & Jewels," as well as being on faculty at two different colleges and an arts center in the Seattle area.

Meredith's main goal as a teacher is to make sure her students are successful and that they enjoy their learning process in her classes. You can see more of her work on her website: www.mereditharnold.com

Olena Bugrimenko is a freelance designer specializing in bead crafting. About eight years ago it was simply a nice hobby for her. Then she started to make handmade jewelry and bead bouquets as birthday presents for her friends. But when she started being recognized in a variety of contests and fairs, including winning the prize from Michael's Create A Sparkle Bead Contest, she began to take her art more seriously. Her inspiration comes from lace, ribbon, or haute couture dresses. She likes to explore combinations of beads and glass with gems and pearls. She tries to combine intricate design with different forms and shapes to add to the originality of each piece. Contact via her website: www.sparklingfantasy.com

Jean Campbell designs, teaches, and writes about beadwork. She is the founding editor of *Beadwork* magazine and has written and edited more than 45 books, most recently including *Beading Inspired by Art: Impressionism, Beading Inspired by Art: Art Nouveau* (with Judith Durant), and the upcoming *Steampunk Style Jewelry*.

Jean is a Crystallized Elements Ambassador for the Swarovski company, and currently writes a popular weekly blog on *BeadingDaily.com*. She has appeared on the DIY *Jewelry Making* show, *The Shay Pendray Show*, and PBS's *Beads, Baubles, and Jewels* where she gives how-to instructions, provides inspiration, and lends crafting advice. Jean teaches off-loom beading throughout the United States. She lives in Minneapolis, Minnesota, with her family and a whole lot of beads. Visit Jean's website at www.jeancampbellink.com.

Geri Cook, along with her husband, is the owner of Beadweavers, located in Louisville, Kentucky. She has been beading for 10 years and teaching for two. Geri teaches all the basic seed bead stitches in addition to beginner stringing. Her shop caters to those new to beading. Best known for her patience with beginners, Geri has a loyal following of students who continually bring in friends and family members for classes. When not beading or pricing beads for her shop, Geri enjoys sewing, tole painting, and playing video games to relax.

Albina Manning really enjoys creating beaded and wirework jewelry, flowers, and décor pieces that bring an unusual atmosphere into the home. She is a professional teacher with 9 years of experience, and began her bead teaching career at the Bead Museum in Glendale. In her classes she shows her students the tricks of trade, so it will be easy for them to make any project. She keeps in touch with her students and is always happy to see them again in her classes.

You can visit her web-site at www.around-beads.info or send her email at albina73@cox.net.

Kathy St Martin has a vast history within the jewelry industry, spanning almost 30 years. As a bead shop owner, Kathy concentrated on the finer aspects of purchasing and learning to tweak her jewelry teaching skills. Now, Kathy is concentrated on establishing the non-profit Mt. Pleasant Art Institute, in Harrisburg, Pennsylvania, which will provide instruction in high quality jewelry and other media to "at risk" women and young adults. For more information call 814-441-0763 or contact her through the Derry Street UMC in Harrisburg, Pennsylvania.

Lana May recalls admiring her grandmother's beaded bride's purse as a child in Uzbekistan. She received her first degree in mechanical engineering and a second degree in clothing and accessory design, then owned a clothing-design firm and began designing jewelry to wear with her evening wear. She now lives in Phoenix, Arizona, and teaches at her home studio, in the Phoenix area, and during the Tucson J.O.G.S. show every year. Visit Lana's website: www. lana-bead.info.

Laurie Nessel wanted to be an artist since her youth when she experimented with photography and ceramics. She received a B.S. from the University of Wisconsin-River Falls in 1978 studying Fibers and Glass. Since then she's been making stained glass windows. She started flameworking in the fall of 1998 and studied under many artists including Janis Miltenberger, Loren Stump, Bill Rasmussen, Pati Walton, Leah Fairbanks, Steve Sizelove, Eli Aller, and Kate Meleney. Since May 2005, she has run the glass studio at the Mesa Arts Center in Mesa, Arizona, and teaches flameworking, including a class for youths. She is inspired by the plants and wildlife she encounters in her adopted Sonoran Desert and expresses this in digital photography and watercolors as well. www.laurienessel.com

Irina Serbina has loved macramé ever since she learned its basics when she was 12. She lived in Ukraine at that time. She began by making some for fun, then made some for friends. Eventually she made a living from her macramé, teaching classes and designing accessories and interior decoration pieces. A resident of California for the past 10 years, she almost got used to the crazy pace of life... and then it hit her: Where is the fun in her life? Where is that beauty that was supposed to save the world? Did she really want to do business consulting for 10-14 hours a day? So she did it: she set out to search for a beauty in the warmth of a stone, in the impeccable form, in the play of light, in the unique combination of materials. She would like you to be the judge; did she find it? Is she close? Is she even going in the right direction? She just hopes you will enjoy her art as much as she enjoys it. Her website: www.macrameboutique.com.

Tatiana Van Iten was born and raised in Russia, where she graduated from the Leningrad State University with a Master of Arts degree in photojournalism. Twenty years ago she married an American citizen and moved to the United States. Tatiana learned the art of beading from her grandmother, at the age of six, and has been beading ever since then.

All instructors teach at the Tucson J.O.G.S. Show every February. You can register on line at www.ArtBeadCircle.com.

J.O.G.S. Gem and Jewelry Show

J.O.G.S. Gem and Jewelry Show is the largest and most popular independent jewelry trade show in the Tucson, Arizona, area. Wholesale jewelry manufacturers, miners and international dealers gather at the Tucson Expo Center, where buyer attendance at the J.O.G.S. show exceeds 27,000, composing over 4,000 jewelry firms.

A truly one-of-a-kind Southwestern jewelry pavilion can be found at the J.O.G.S. show. It includes great Mexican and Native American designs of turquoise and coral set in silver. The top dealers, miners, and manufacturers from Albuquerque, Mexico, and China attend with their large stock of jewelry.

At the J.O.G.S. Gem Show, the largest U.S. amber jewelry pavilions presented by the American Amber Association. The pavilion includes amber designers and amber manufacturers from all the Baltic countries famous for their amber source. If you are an amber retailer or are just an amber-holic, you will love this pavilion. The J.O.G.S. show is your once-a-year opportunity to buy these great designs at excellent prices.

The Art Gem Décor pavilion contains some of the most beautiful décor items crafted from stones, gems, copper, wood, metal, and other materials. These are museum quality pieces created by some of the most talented artists in the world. This is truly one of the most unique art collections you will ever see. It is like an art show inside the J.O.G.S. show. Besides the exquisite art pieces, you can also find some great everyday interior design pieces.

Other J.O.G.S. Gem Show pavilions include the many international pavilions which represent the rich gem and jewelry heritage of Indonesia, Hong Kong, Thailand, Mexico, and Nepal.

There are products at the J.O.G.S. show to suit just about any buyer. The range covers all price points, from high end, one-of-a-kind designs to everyday popular items available at wholesale prices. Often buyers rely on the expertise of the wholesale sellers to pick out next season's hottest selling lines. Buyers can be seen purchasing large quantities at wholesale prices as well as occasional one-of-a-kind purchases intended for personal and private collections.

At the state-of-the-art Tucson Expo Center, the whole show takes place under one roof and on the same floor, ensuring that buyers visit every booth and no vendor gets left out. Great promotion, a complimentary lunch buffet for the buyers, top security and a red carpet atmosphere has been responsible for the success of the J.O.G.S. show.

Many supplies for this book were provided by firemountaingems.com.